BATTLING
FOR THE
MODERN MIND

G. K. Chesterton

BATTLING
FOR THE
MODERN MIND

A Beginner's Chesterton

Thomas C. Peters

CPH
SAINT LOUIS

Copyright © 1994 Concordia Publishing House
3558 S. Jefferson Avenue, St. Louis, MO 63118-3968
Manufactured in the United States of America

Library of Congress Cataloging-in-Publication Data

Peters, Thomas C., 1948–
    Battling for the modern mind : a beginner's Chesterton / Thomas C. Peters.
       p.   cm.   —(Concordia scholarship today)
    ISBN 0-570-04664-5
    1. Chesterton, G. K. (Gilbert Keith), 1874–1936. 2. Apologetics—History—20th century. 3. Catholic Church—Apologetic works—History—20th century. I. Title. II. Series.
BT1117.P47   1994
230'.2'092—dc20   94-5963

1 2 3 4 5 6 7 8 9 10   03 02 01 00 99 98 97 96 95 94

Dedicated with love and hope
to
Samuel Thomas Peters

Contents

Foreword

The battle for the mind dates back to Genesis 3, when the first human beings lost the battle and left a bequest with dire consequences that still plague us. They failed to recognize their protagonist, the nature of the confrontation, or its significance. Today, millennia later, the confusion persists. Countless words continue to be written in what seems to be a fruitless effort to single out causes for the problems that frustrate society and the world.

Some progress might be forthcoming if we could agree that in the final analysis all problems grow out of a battle for the mind and, more specifically, for the will. Nietzsche's notion of a universal "will for power" was valid insofar as he identified the strength of that aspect of the mind which, no matter how powerful or obvious, determines action (or inaction). Yet many political interpreters tend not to recognize political conflict for what it is—a battle for the mind, for the will. Similar conditions also contribute to economic, social, and even spiritual problems, producing confusion, disarray, and turmoil. How many well-written and accurate analyses of the symptoms stop short of identifying the ultimate cause or determinant: the idea (the mind, the will)!

To be sure, symptoms cannot be ignored. They must be analyzed. Solutions must be weighed and tried. But, ultimately, ideas—those that generate the problems and those that support the proposed solutions—have consequences. The countless analyses of current issues alone defy reading by any single person, not to mention the recommended remedies or the same menu from past history.

For that reason Thomas C. Peters originally wrote *Battling for the Modern Mind* for the day when his 10-year-old son would encounter the spiritual and moral milieu of the 21st century. His son could benefit from practical advice when confronted with the confusing—and often conflicting—intellectual environment he would soon face. Fascinated with the writings of G. K. Chesterton, a contemporary of C. S. Lewis—and his mentor (so Lewis said)—Peters chose to offer samples from Chesterton, with appropriate comment, rather than simply suggesting, "Read Chesterton." The result is delightful reading, not only for the entering college student, but also for the mature reader already acquainted with Chesterton.

Three thousand years ago the writer of Ecclesiastes said, "Of making many books there is no end" (12:12). What would he say today about our age and its proliferation of books—not to mention the books about the books! What books should we then read? Inviting the reader to plumb the thinking of the past, as author Peters does, is a rising trend, while the popularity of deconstructionism and other efforts to disparage the wisdom of the past (mercifully) decline. Leaders in the new movement include distinguished thinkers, among them Thomas C. Oden (*After Modernity . . . What?*), who heralds the "profound rediscovery of the texts and wisdom of the long-neglected patristic pastoral tradition," as well as other classic writings since then that provide guidance and balance for our postmodern world. By recommending Chesterton as worthwhile reading for the continuing battle for the mind and by supplying discerning analyses of his writings, Thomas C. Peters has rendered his readers a valuable service.

The Publisher

1

Discovering Chesterton

"This book makes no pretense to be anything but a popular sketch of a great historical character who ought to be more popular," wrote G. K. Chesterton in the introduction to his biography of Saint Thomas Aquinas. The same is true of the book you are now holding in your hands. For my intention here is not to write a scholarly paper, nor even a biography, but something closer to a popular sketch of the writings and thoughts of another great historical character: Gilbert Keith Chesterton.

Now as we approach the third millennium of the Christian era, we can look back on the two most recent centuries with a sense of wonder at the tremendous changes that men and women have wrought in their relations with their environment and with each other. In historical perspective we can truly say that at mid-19th century, the flames of scientific discovery and technological invention flared rapidly into a bonfire of innovation, which is still blazing vigorously and bringing profound changes into the everyday lives of people everywhere.

But some have suggested that the fire is out of control and threatens to destroy us in its proud and irresponsible fury. Certainly the ubiquitous threat of nuclear annihilation and the specter of global pollution add credence to this view. Others have said that the wildfire has damaged us in more subtle, but even more important ways—having to do with the minds, the hearts, and the souls of modern men and women. Since its brilliant rise to eminence, the establishment of scientific and commercial progress has seen its moral detractors, its romantic dissenters, its poets and prophets crying in the wilderness. Far from the least among these poet-prophets was G. K. Chesterton.

The importance of G. K. Chesterton at the dawning of the third millennium lies in the fact that he and the modern era literally came of age together. It was during his own formative years that the greatest strides were made in technology and industry, and as a young man he was already immersed in the popular ideologies that came to characterize the 20th century.

But Chesterton's was a mind awake. He did not let progressive enthusiasms blind him to the inhuman effects of urban-industrial trends—the displacement of the poor, the high unemployment, the wretched slum conditions, and more. Nor did he let intellectual fashions blind him to the logical and ethical poverty of the most popular ideas—the agnostic skepticism, the free-floating relativism, the evolutionary progressivism, and more. Against the current of opinion, G. K. Chesterton soon began to question publicly the very foundations of the institutions and ideologies that so many considered splendidly modern and inevitable.

And today, as the moral and spiritual bankruptcy of the 20th century becomes increasingly inescapable, people find themselves asking the troubling questions: How did things come to be this way? Where did we go wrong? Where do we go from here? Indeed, the agnosticism, the skepticism, the materialism, the relativism, and the progressivism have run their course; and people are discovering that they do not like the course they have run. But I am sorry to say that they have simply run the course that G. K. Chesterton had predicted they would run.

It is, in fact, the perfect time to go back and look at what G. K. Chesterton was saying. If his insight and wisdom were not widely heeded during his lifetime, there is still no reason to think that they cannot be heeded now. For Chesterton's ideas do specifically address those three troubling, modern questions. There are answers and there are solutions, but only for those souls who are brave enough to turn around and look back. There will always be a chance for renewal, if only we can stop and take responsibility for what we have done.

I wonder how many times over how many years in my reading I skimmed across the words, "As G. K. Chesterton once said . . . ," and entertained a vague thought that I ought some day to read Chesterton firsthand. But now having feasted at Chesterton's raucous and jolly table for some time, I am certain that I should have been introduced to his books long ago.

For now I have discovered for myself the solid insights, the clear logic, the razor-sharp wit, and the brawling humor of this great and memorable man. And now, perhaps with a naivete and zeal typical of the novice, it is my humble purpose here to urge and help others to become beginners in the world of G. K. Chesterton as well.

G. K. Chesterton is widely known as one of the most effective and entertaining defenders of the Christian faith in the early part of the 20th century. Through the tangled jungle of modern philosophies, doctrines, and notions, Chesterton blazed a broad path encompassing several genres. He was a career journalist; the London newspapers and journals were blessed with steady dosages of Chesterton essays on subjects both religious and nonreligious. He was a writer of detective stories—notably his very popular Father Brown series—as well as a few novels. He wrote nonfiction commentaries on Thomas Aquinas, Francis of Assisi, William Blake, Robert Louis Stevenson, George Bernard Shaw, and Charles Dickens, to name a few. And he was a highly popular lecturer and debater throughout his native England.

But Chesterton had not always been a Christian believer. He was not raised on strong Christian instruction, nor did he consider himself a Christian believer during his early adult years. In his book *Orthodoxy,* Chesterton traced the journey of his heart and intellect from an early acceptance of the agnostic materialism of the age, through a series of discoveries and changes, and eventually to the conclusion that the doctrines of orthodox Christian faith made the most sense of all.

> I tried to be some ten minutes in advance of the truth. And I found that I was eighteen hundred years behind it. . . . I have kept my truths; but I have discovered, not that they were not truths, but simply that they were not mine. When I fancied that I stood alone I was really in the ridiculous position of being backed up by all Christendom. . . . I did try to found a heresy of my own; and when I had put the last touches to it, I discovered that it was orthodox.[1]

Throughout his writing, Chesterton used the word "orthodoxy" simply to mean Christian doctrine as defined in the Apostles' Creed.

The author G. K. Chesterton is difficult to classify, because he expressed himself in so many varied ways in so many different forums. His efforts defy the label "religious writings," for most of his writing was not about religion or theology in the usual senses of the terms. He was indeed a social commentator—or perhaps what we in the United States today would call a syndicated columnist—but he was also a good part the philosopher, the ethicist, the sociologist, the historian, the political activist, and the teller of tales. Perhaps after all we can call him a religious writer, but in that more profound sense of religion as embracing the very human intersections of doctrine and the everyday realities of living in the world.

Consequently, in Chesterton's writings one seldom finds quotations of Scripture, and even more rarely exegesis thereon. One in fact seldom enough finds discussions of Christian doctrine at all. And yet, as one enjoys the various essays, speeches, and stories of G. K. Chesterton, one begins to realize a deeper consistency, a strong movement in a certain direction, and that direction turns out to be a statement of the reality and meaning of the life, death, and resurrection of Jesus of Nazareth in conflict with the major, popular notions and creeds of the 20th century.

Because of this very basic conflict, G. K. Chesterton was forever involved in controversy. His journalism contained his tireless forays against the giants and dragons which he saw marauding England and other modern states—political corruption, industrial exploitation, irresponsible capitalism, dehumanizing socialism, scientific determinism, materialist philosophy, and a host of follies hidden in vague and popular phrases like "survival of the fittest" and "progress" and in the growing rejection of all tradition.

But to call the ideas of G. K. Chesterton conservative or reactionary would be simplistic and inaccurate. One may just as well call them liberal or radical. For as Chesterton so often and so gaily pointed out, his was not a reactionary call back to some former state of life, but rather a radical call to a new state of life which was defined long ago but has as yet never been tried:

> [T]he great ideals of the past failed not by being outlived ... but by not being lived enough. Mankind has not passed through the Middle Ages. Rather mankind has retreated from the Middle Ages in reaction and rout. The Christian ideal has not been tried and found wanting. It has been found difficult; and left untried.[2]

G. K. Chesterton was ever the controversialist, and as such he spent the majority of his public life locked in verbal and written combat against many of the major intellectuals of his day. In print he would cheerfully lambast the Fabian Socialist ideas of his dear

14

friend, George Bernard Shaw. In lecture he would merrily ridicule the scientific determinism of another friend, H. G. Wells. He was an unceasing critic of unsupportable nonsense masquerading as science, of the faulty logic of many learned experts, and of the deadening effects of Puritan legalism in religion and politics.

But only half the joy in reading Chesterton lies in what he argued; the other half lies in how he argued. Particularly in his debates with George Bernard Shaw, the combatants often good-naturedly said the most derogatory things about the other's logic and thoughts. G.K.C. might say, "For the truth is that Mr. Shaw has never seen things as they really are,"[3] to which Shaw might smile and respond with some equal slander of Chesterton's mental capacities. Acquaintances said of Chesterton that he appeared genuinely to love all people, but that he did not feel therefore compelled to like their ideas.

Many modern, liberal, "open minded" readers will no doubt consider some of Chesterton's ideas offensive and perhaps backward. For the popular modern ethos calls for a vague relativism that is tolerant of many and varied points of view, and that becomes uneasy when someone simply believes and defends a fixed point of view—particularly if that view happens to be in some sense traditional. Today one who defends an old creed is likely to be dismissed as a closed-minded dogmatist, a prejudiced fanatic, or even a bigot.

Such charges cannot be dismissed lightly, because I think that many, if not most, modern readers of G.K.C. are apt to feel uneasy along similar lines. For sure, Chesterton was a highly opinionated man and a forceful debater. In reading his books one can hardly avoid the witty stab of Chesterton's sword pricking the skin of certain favorite ideas. G.K.C. was forever making surprising arguments in favor of unpopular ideas and against popular ones. That is at least part of the attraction in reading G. K. Chesterton.

But to dismiss a man of Chesterton's breadth and brilliance as merely "prejudiced" or "bigoted" would be the grossest injustice. Few men have ever been less so. If to be prejudiced is to prejudge, to form opinions without bothering with the facts, then one needs only to read Chesterton's essays to realize the factual and logical bases of his arguments. One may vehemently disagree with the man's conclusions, but one cannot fairly accuse G.K.C. of prejudice.

What many modern people forget is that to stand on the "wrong" side of an argument is not the same thing as to be prejudiced.

And if a bigot is one who is so obstinately attached to an opinion as to be illiberal or intolerant, one needs only to read G. K. Chesterton's *Autobiography* to follow a mind working its way from one end of the philosophical spectrum to the opposite end. His was a mind open to experience, to logic, and even to tradition in his perpetual search for truth.

To have thought and have come to firm conclusions, and to have defended those conclusions with all his might and wit, does not make the man a bigot. It merely means that he was fortunate enough in his thinking to have come to some conclusions. In this connection a question arises. Who is the more illiberal: the person who studies and thinks and argues and raves about his conclusions, or the one who summarily dismisses the author of unfriendly conclusions? As G.K.C. himself often pointed out, sometimes "freethinkers" can be quite illiberal.

As a matter of fact, Chesterton had a lot to say about the "free-thinkers" of his day. One comment was this:

> [A] freethinker does not mean a man who thinks for himself. It means a man who, having thought for himself, has come to one particular class of conclusions, the material origin of phenomena, the impossibility of miracles, the improbability of personal immortality, and so on. And none of these ideas are particularly liberal. Nay, almost all these ideas are definitely illiberal.[4]

Much of the pleasure in reading G.K.C. is the sheer enjoyment of a verbal banquet. Chesterton bit into ideas and chewed them rigorously. His thoughts were not tentative nor relative; he was not one to equivocate. His mode of discussion was defense and offense; he did not pretend value-free analysis. In his fiction he was fond of sword fighting; in his nonfiction he was equally fond of face-to-face combat.

I have mentioned Chesterton's propensity sooner or later to step on one's toes. I first found him stepping on my toes on doctrinal grounds. For G.K.C. was an ardent, militant Roman Catholic, and I am on the other hand a seriously committed Protestant. For certain, the Protestant reader does find challenges in Chesterton's writings. G.K.C. made no secret of the fact that he considered Protestantism itself to be an objectionable modern version of an ancient heresy that the Roman Catholic Church had rejected long ago.

Consequently, the Protestant reader is compelled to absorb the occasional missile from Chesterton's arsenal, even if at times his remarks seem a bit unfair. He might remark in passing on "Luther's frank paganism" or the "prison" of Calvin's Puritanism,[5] or even more combatively:

> There were sincere ideals in some of the early Protestants; but they are not the ideals of any of the modern Protestants. . . . The genuine Protestant creed is now hardly held by anyone—least of all by Protestants. So completely have they lost faith in it, that they have mostly forgotten what it was.[6]

As uncomfortable as such thrusts may make us feel, even such pointed criticisms can be put to good use. For as any honest Protestant must admit, there is a great amount of folly parading around under the banner of Protestant Christianity, and—without descending into the fruitless argument of whether Protestants or Roman Catholics harbor the greatest foolishness—much can be gained from paying close attention to our intelligent critics. One can heartily disagree with Chesterton's assessment of Protestantism on doctrinal grounds, and yet one can only laugh along at some of the specific follies he so merrily attacked.

But in fact, Chesterton's critiques of Protestant doctrine were not his central theme; his mind and energies were largely engaged with the broader and more destructive forces of the age. G. K. Chesterton's lifetime of work stands as a bold and heroic challenge to the oncoming tide of secularism, atheism, materialism, skepticism, economic and scientific determinism, and inhumanity in the name of progress. And so, recognizing that Christians, Protestant and Roman Catholic, have much more in common than in difference, I came to appreciate G.K.C. for the Christian banner he did champion in the face of the colossal and seemingly inexorable forces that have been shaping modern Western societies.

But back to the small question. "How can I believe any of this book, if I can't believe all of it?" I was asked this question by a young girl who did not know any better, but I am afraid that there are far too many adults who should know better, but do not. I have often heard in religious settings this curious and unrealistic doctrine of all-or-nothing, as if a person's statements must be all true or all false. Similarly, many Protestants will ask, "How can I believe the insights of Chesterton, when he is so wrong about something as important as our Protestant doctrines?"

The answer, of course, is that one must never simply, uncritically "believe" every thought of any other person, no matter who he or she may be. G. K. Chesterton was simply a human being—albeit an exceptionally intelligent one—just as were other great Christian writers like Augustine, Aquinas, Pascal, Martin Luther, John Calvin, John Newman, Thomas Merton, and C. S. Lewis. It would be sheer folly to hand one's rational judgment on every important question over to any fellow mortal, no matter how brilliant or famous he or she may be.

Incidentally, the Protestant writer C. S. Lewis was at times rather critical of the Roman Catholic Church, but a great many Roman Catholics have enjoyed and benefited from Lewis' fiction and non-fiction through the years. And I am certain that both Lewis and Chesterton would roar with indignation at the thought of anyone "believing in" their every word in the first place. "Use your mind! Think it through, yourself!" they would both no doubt bellow.

In this regard, Chesterton often wrote about the dangers of believing men of intellect—of which G.K.C. was most certainly one—no matter what banner they may wave. For example,

> It did not seem to occur to such controversialists that if Cardinal Newman was really a man of intellect, the fact that he adhered to dogmatic religion proved exactly as much as the fact that Professor Huxley, another man of intellect, found that he could not adhere to dogmatic religion; that is to say (as I cheerfully admit), it proved precious little either way. If there is one class of men whom history has proved especially and supremely capable of going quite wrong in all directions, it is the class of highly intellectual men.[7]

The point was not to ignore the thoughts of the highly intelligent, but always to weight them in the scales of one's own rational faculties and common sense.

One of the very reasons I am compiling this book is to introduce young readers to the wit and logic of this remarkable Catholic writer. Denominational differences aside, the works of Chesterton are every bit as essential, as insightful, as important to solid Christian underpinnings as those of the popular Protestant writer, C. S. Lewis. In fact, Lewis himself thought very highly of Chesterton, and many quotations from G.K.C. appear throughout the writings of C. S. Lewis.

Once a reader becomes acquainted with Chesterton, it is amazing to see how frequently and widely the man is quoted in print. The reason is simply that Chesterton had a delightful way with words. His fervent purposes and lucid insights were expressed so imaginatively and with such joyful relish as to carry his readers along in the momentum of his enthusiasm. His statements often leave one saying, "That is so true! I had never thought of putting it that way!"

In this beginner's guide, we endeavor to tour the mind of G. K. Chesterton. We begin appropriately with a look at his sense of humor, for it was his wit and his sense of play that characterized the man possibly to a greater extent than any other of his remarkable traits. Next we revisit his life, paying particular attention to his *Autobiography*. And finally we begin to explore Chesterton's main interests and themes through a review of his fiction, including his short stories and especially his novels.

The heart of Chesterton's nonfiction efforts in the fields of philosophy, sociology, and politics appears in the next three chapters. "Resisting the Spell" discusses Chesterton's thoughts on materialist philosophy, skepticism, scientific determinism, and the concept of progress. The chapter called "Jousting with the Giant" deals with G.K.C.'s responses to pseudo-scientific dogma and superstition, relativism, the popular attacks against tradition and authority, and the various modern attempts at scientific management of public policy. Finally, "Tilting at Dragons" discusses Chesterton's ideas in politics, including his advocacy of "distributism" and his opposition to imperialism, plutocracy, and corruption in government.

The final two chapters are more directly concerned with Chesterton's religious ideas. "Consorting in Fairyland" outlines his sacramental view of life and includes more of his arguments against materialist philosophy. The final chapter, "Getting to the Heart of Matters," attempts to summarize Chesterton's theology, which is after all the mainspring of all his philosophical, social, and political ideas.

G. K. Chesterton was a man of many talents and various, surprising aspects. He was highly intelligent and extremely witty, as the reader will discover in the following pages. He was romantic in the truest and broadest sense of the word. And he was passionate—for he had a burning desire to free himself and his fellow human beings from the slavery that he saw lurking behind the most popular ideas of the 20th century. He was great in his ideas, his arguments, and his roaring attempts to save his fellows; and yet he was humble and counted himself among the least. In this profound sense, G. K. Chesterton was a Christian.

2

Hearing God's Laughter

If there is one word that captures the character of G. K. Chesterton, I think the word is laughter. G.K.C. was a man who laughed easily and uproariously, a man who truly enjoyed the social intercourse of men and women as well as the verbal interplay of ideas great and small. He was a man ready to laugh, because he found so much in the world to laugh about. His very thoughts of heaven were of a great playground, and his thoughts of God amounted to a theology of joy.

"Heaven does not work; it plays," he wrote,[1] and he often gave the impression that what was truly essential to God was an overwhelming sense of joy. In the life and writings of Chesterton one sees a man responding in gratitude and joy to his Creator, a man seizing the best that the Creator offers—a full measure of the life, the love, and the laughter for which we were all created.

Chesterton never tired of pointing out that men and women were made in the image of God. This point was an indispensable part of Chesterton's theology, because it became the logical foundation for many of his arguments in politics, economics, sociology, and philosophy. It was also essential to his explanation of our comedies and our laughter. He wrote,

> Why is it funny that a man should sit down suddenly in the street? There is only one possible or intelligent reason: that man is the image of God. . . . Why do we laugh? Because it is a grave religious matter: it is the Fall of Man. Only man can be absurd: for only man can be dignified.[2]

In another context he explained, "All the jokes about men sitting down on their hats are really theological jokes; they are concerned with the Dual Nature of Man. They refer to the primary paradox that man is superior to all the things around him and yet is at their mercy."[3]

But in Chesterton's view being created in the image of God

carried with it another implication: that people at their best are at least flawed replications of their Creator. In this regard the New Testament included joy among the fruit of the Spirit of God;[4] it is fair to say that Chesterton capitalized on the joy of God. One of his enduring concerns as an author was the nurturance and preservation of the joy which was intended for the people of God.

G.K.C. was fond of writing verse and rhyme, although he never considered himself particularly adept at the craft. One can see most clearly his instinctual mirth in many of his playful rhymes, particularly in the collection called *Greybeards at Play*. For example, in a short poem called "Triolet" he wrote

> I wish I were a jelly fish
> That cannot fall downstairs:
> Of all the things I wish to wish
> I wish I were a jelly fish
> That hasn't any cares,
> And doesn't even have to wish
> "I wish I were a jelly fish
> That cannot fall downstairs."[5]

It is essential to realize that Chesterton was serious about mirth and laughter. It was a matter of great importance to him that God created humans for joy, and this assertion was, in fact, the basis of Chesterton's continuous railing against the deadening effects of modern society. Thus, his jolly wordplay was not merely a diversion, but more of an assertion of levity into a world which appeared to be straining under the weight of taking itself far too seriously.

In another rhyme titled "Of the Dangers Attending Altruism on the High Seas" he wrote,

> I am, I think I have remarked
>   Terrifically old,
> (The second Ice-age was a farce,
>   The first was rather cold.)[6]

This joy in language is one of the very things that makes reading G. K. Chesterton so pleasurable, for even his serious essays are adorned with these delightful little surprises. One might be seriously engaged with his arguments regarding the philosophical effects of certain themes in modern drama, only to unearth suddenly a sparkling gem like, "It will be a happy day in the dramatic world when all ladies have to take off their hats and all critics have to take off their heads."[7]

We are told that many of his contemporary critics found such levities at least an irritating distraction, if not evidence of his insincerity in debate. But as one reaches more thoroughly into Chesterton's thoughts, one sees that his sense of play was an infinitely more "solemn" matter than his critics must have realized. Chesterton wrote,

> But it has been possible, and it will be possible again, for the public to rejoice seriously, and even solemnly. In those older days the very word "solemn" went with the word "joyous"; and "a high solemnity" was almost always an affair of dancing and junketing.[8]

This sense of the solemnity of play and laughter permeates Chesterton's fiction and nonfiction alike. He wrote, "... man is a very comic creature, and most of the things he does are comic,"[9] and again with regard to play,

> ... but I for one have never left off playing, and I wish there were more time to play. I wish we did not have to fritter away on frivolous things, like lectures and literature, the time we might have given to serious, solid and constructive work like cutting out cardboard figures and pasting coloured tinsel upon them.[10]

And yet even more,

> It might reasonably be maintained that the true object of all human life is play. Earth is a task garden; heaven is a playground. To be at last in such secure innocence that one can juggle with the universe and stars, to be so good that one can treat everything as a joke—that may be, perhaps, the real end and final holiday of human souls. When we are really holy we may regard the Universe as a lark . . . .[11]

In Chesterton's view the comic—laughter, song, merriment, nonsense verse, romance, imagination, play—was central to the relationship between God and humanity. The human life properly lived might be called a "solemn and joyous occasion"; a person's contemplations of God a theology of joy.

In his irrepressible zeal for human life lived to its fullest, Chesterton declared a holy war against the forces in modern society that sought to stifle the joys of the people. In this regard he was forever critical of the pretensions and conceits of high society—of the powerful, the rich, the famous, and the intellectual elite. In response to a complaint that Oxford University was little more than a playground for the governing class, Chesterton made the rather surprising reply, "I would much rather be ruled by men who know how to play than by men who do not know how to play."[12] It was the important men and women who did not know how to play, who took themselves far too seriously, for whom Chesterton reserved some of his most biting observations.

Nowadays we do not often hear the word "prig" as Chesterton often used it. A prig generally is one who irritates by proprieties observed to an obnoxious degree—one whom we might today call a pretentious snob. G.K.C. was particularly hard on "prigs," as can be seen in his analysis of the "priggish" habit of some to make sneering "private jokes" about their social inferiors.

> The old idea that the joke was not good enough for the company has been superseded by the new aristocratic idea that the company was not worthy of the joke. They have introduced an almost insane individualism into that one form of intercourse which is specially and uproariously communal. They have made even levities into secrets. They have made laughter lonelier than tears.[13]

But most of the blame for robbing modern society of its God-given joy Chesterton laid at the feet of the Puritans. Puritanism, according to G.K.C., presented a God who was a sort of cosmic kill-joy and mortals whose duty it was to maintain a "sour vigilance that would arrest the amusements of the populace."[14] The problem as Chesterton saw it was that Puritanism had lost its religion but retained its petty morals:

> Thus I, for one, regret the supersession of the old Puritan unity, founded on theology, but embracing all types from Milton to the grocer, by that newer Puritan unity which is founded rather on certain social habits, certain common notions, both permissive and prohibitive, in connection with particular social pleasures.[15]

What Chesterton found most obnoxious in Puritan moral standards were primarily the petty prohibitions, which he believed to be arbitrary and theologically unfounded. He reacted to the Puritan moralists much as Jesus reacted to the scribes and Pharisees who "tie up heavy loads and lay them on men's shoulders."[16] Chesterton wrote, "Nothing is needed, for most of their moral movements, but a sort of gesture of priggish repugnance and small-minded superiority; and it would be just as easy for a moralist to make that sort of face over a jar of pickles as over a pot of porter."[17]

Chesterton's chief complaint against Puritanism had to do with misplaced vigilance and arbitrary morals. There was a sense in his writing that he suspected such moralists of deliberately opposing enjoyment for the sake of opposing enjoyment. He quoted Macaulay as saying that "the Puritans hated bear-baiting, not because it gave pain to the bear, but because it gave pleasure to the spectators."[18] And it was surely Chesterton's intention to fly in the face of Puritan teetotalism with his playful rhyme about the biblical patriarch Noah:

> Old Noah he had an ostrich farm
>   and fowls on the largest scale,
> He ate his eggs with a ladle
>   in an egg-cup big as a pail,
> And the soup he took was Elephant Soup
>   and the fish he took was Whale,
> But they all were small to the cellar
>   he took when he set out to sail,
> And Noah he often said to his wife
>   when he sat down to dine,
> "I don't care where the water goes
>   if it doesn't get into the wine."[19]

The new Puritanism, in Chesterton's words, "produces a mood which does darken the world,"[20] and as such it drew some of his heaviest verbal fire.

But the theology of joy in Chesterton's writing became most visible in his arguments against the skeptics, the cynics, the pessimists in modern thought. Some of his most impassioned writing occurred when he was countering the claims that life is not worth living or that there is nothing to be happy about. These arguments will be discussed in some detail in a later chapter; but briefly, G.K.C. argued that if people are indeed free individuals capable of moral decisions, then it is their responsibility to make the choices that will bring them joy.

> For it is always wiser to consider not so much why a thing is not enjoyable, as why we ourselves do not enjoy it.[21]

25

In other words, God created us capable of joy, and God created much around us for our enjoyment. In Chesterton's view, wisdom would have us look to ourselves if we fail to find the world enjoyable.

The sacredness of play and romance is a major recurrent theme in much of Chesterton's writing, and particularly in his fiction. It is a theme that is developed to some extent in his novel *The Flying Inn*, but is developed even more fully in *Manalive*. In both novels, Chesterton's main protagonists personify the kind of radical seizing of life, the living of the sacrament of joy, that was so central to Chesterton's view of human life.

The Flying Inn is a playful, rollicking novel that follows the adventures of Patrick Dalroy and his innkeeper friend Humphrey Pump as they evade a series of new laws designed to deprive the English lower classes of alcoholic beverage. It is a novel in which G.K.C. took a satiric swipe at several of his favorite targets among the popular aristocratic fads of the day—including prohibition, vegetarianism, pacifism, pantheism, the worship of progress, hypocritical diplomacy, and the vague admiration of anything and everything of oriental origin.

Chesterton introduced a great amount of wordplay into *The Flying Inn* through the drinking songs of Dalroy and Pump. Humphrey Pump is former proprietor of "The Old Ship," a traditional English inn, which was driven out of business by restrictive laws and the advent of a new phenomenon called the grocery store. In a moment of melancholy, Pump invents "The Song Against Grocers." Here is a sample:

> God made the wicked Grocer
> For a mystery and a sign,
> That men might shun the awful shops
> And go to inns to dine;
> Where the bacon's on the rafter
> And the wine is in the wood,
> And God that made good laughter
> Has seen that they are good.[22]

The grocer is not simply meant as the target of an unhappy innkeeper; he is clearly a symbol for something that Chesterton found threatening to the good of the English people—the systematic and progressive curtailment of the real human contacts as found in the old English inns. The bacon and the wine and the good laughter of the inn represent all of the pleasure and cameraderie that God intended for people to enjoy in the company of friends.

More of Chesterton's play comes in the form of a song supposedly written by the dog, Quoodle, on the subject of humans' stunted sense of smell:

> They haven't got no noses,
> The fallen sons of Eve;
> Even the smell of roses
> Is not what they supposes;
> But more than mind discloses
> And more than men believe.[23]

And again as in so much of Chesterton's foolery, there is a purpose after all. For in this case the rhyme reflects one of the author's central themes: that there is, indeed, much more to reality than modern people are willing to perceive or believe.

But *The Flying Inn* contains much more than random wordplay and selected satire. It is a novel that reflects the author's heartfelt rebellion against the flow of machine-age life toward machine-like life. Early in the story, the young woman Joan Brett asks vaguely of the innkeeper Humphrey Pump, "Oh, Hump, do you think any of us will ever be happy again?"[24] The novel *The Flying Inn* is about the very things that made its author wonder if England should ever be happy again.

Chesterton's noisy defense of alcoholic drink seems at first rather curious, until the reader realizes that the author is using alcohol as a symbol. Thus, early in the novel, Dalroy sings his lament for the closing of a favorite inn, "The Saracen's Head."

> "The Saracen's Head" looks down the lane,
> Where we shall never drink wine again,
> For the wicked old women who feel well-bred
> Have turned to a tea-shop "The Saracen's Head."[25]

One might at first imagine this to be a mere complaint against the prohibitionism of Lord Ivywood, until the reader is given a further clue as to what Chesterton is about. His description of Ivywood's watching the destruction of Pump's "The Old Ship" is revealing.

> And he stood for hours on the lawn, watching the smashing of
> bottles and the breaking up of casks, and feeding on fanatical

pleasure: the pleasure which his strange, cold, courageous nature could not get from food or wine or woman.[26]

Here the scheme of symbols and meanings begins to emerge—the cold, fanatical pleasure taken by some who make war against honest God-given pleasures.

But it is important to note that Chesterton was not talking about a mere psychological type; he was most definitely reacting to a cultural flow, a direction in which he saw modern society drifting. Consistent with his lifelong affinity with working people and the unemployed poor, G.K.C. wrote about hypocritical privilege and about the rich imposing unfair burdens on the poor. *The Flying Inn* is really about the inhumanity of those in the driver's seat of modern industrial society.

In one of his many eccentric soliloquies, the novel's protagonist Patrick Dalroy reveals the principle of the elite's norms and laws:

> If they have to choose between beef and pickles, they always abolish the beef. If they have to choose between a meadow and a motor, they forbid the meadow. Shall I tell you the secret? These men only surrender the things that bind them to other men. Go and dine with a temperance millionaire, and you won't find he's abolished the *hors d'oeuvres* or the five courses or even the coffee. What he's abolished is the port and sherry; because poor men like that as well as rich. Go a step farther, and you won't find he's abolished the fine silver forks and spoons; but he's abolished the meat: because poor men like meat—when they can get it.[27]

It is the self-serving laws and notions of the rich that Chesterton so mercilessly satirized in this novel, and against which he fought in his writing and speaking throughout his life.

As to the issue of human joy, Chesterton's novel *The Flying Inn* is a joy to read, but it is even more a protest against all of the important and powerful people who would impose their latest fads—their fashionable philosophies and morals and prohibitions— upon the powerless around them. In the face of all that is dehumanizing, all of the powerful forces that would suppress the human spirit of joy, Patrick Dalroy reasons, "I don't know whether God means a man to have happiness in that All in All and Utterly Utter sense of happiness. But God does mean man to have a little Fun; and I mean to go on having it."[28] *The Flying Inn* was G. K. Chesterton's brawling song of encouragement for modern people to seize the joy for which they were created.

But in considering Chesterton's novels, I judge *Manalive* to be the best. I say this not as one well-versed in the technical criteria known to the literary critic, but as one who simply found *Manalive* to be one of the most meaningful and enjoyable novels I have ever read. It is a book that illustrates the raucous love of life which defines the creed of G. K. Chesterton—his belief that novelty, adventure, humor, and joy are essential ingredients to the sacrament of human life.

As the novel's title indicates, the story is about a man who is truly alive. The mood is set in the book's opening lines:

> A wind sprang high in the west, like a wave of unreasonable happiness, and tore eastward across England .... everywhere it bore drama into undramatic lives.[29]

And these lines become a prophetic description of the effects of Innocent Smith, the main character, on the lives through which he rambles and tumbles in the novel.

Without revealing here the solutions to the novel's delightful puzzles and riddles, I will disclose that the story line follows a highly unusual man on his quest to revive life in a world dying of its own ideas and habits. A character who is sympathetic to Innocent Smith explains the problem this way:

> "All habits are bad habits," said Michael with deadly calm. "Madness does not come by breaking out, but by giving in; by settling down in some dirty, little, self-repeating circle of ideas; by being tamed ...."[30]

Innocent Smith—who is at different points considered an enigma, a madman, a criminal, and a saint—personifies the challenge to the "bad habits" and "circles of ideas" which G. K. Chesterton saw as depriving modern men and women of the joy for which they were created.

Thus, through the adventures of his protagonist, Chesterton confronts scientific positivism in France, Liberal Socialism and Ibsenism in Russia, the Celestial Principles and Confucius in the Orient, reclusive isolationism in America, and finally a deeper appreciation of his own home again in England. And through the fictional trial of Innocent Smith, Chesterton contrasts the ideas of modern criminology and medicine with those of an older creed admitting the free will and moral responsibility of individuals, and the human dignity that comes from having been created in the image of God.

Much of the exposition in *Manalive* is accomplished by a flash-back technique, as the opposing advocates bring evidence in the trial of Innocent Smith for attempted murder, burglary, desertion, and polygamy. Indeed, it is only as the final trial proceeds that the reader begins to piece together the meaningful consistency in Smith's actions. And, as in so much of Chesterton's life and work, that consistency lies in his bold assertion that God created humans for the purpose of living their lives heartily and appreciating their blessings joyfully.

Much of the author's purpose is expressed in the testimonies of the witnesses at Smith's trial:

> His eccentricities sprang from a static fact of faith, in itself mystical, and even childlike and Christian.[31]

> His creed of wonder was Christian by this absolute test; that he felt it continually slipping from himself as much as from others.[32]

> His principle can be quite simply stated: he refuses to die while he is still alive. He seeks to remind himself, by every electric shock to the intellect, that he is still a man alive . . . .[33]

Innocent Smith thus embodies one of G. K. Chesterton's most in-cessant themes: that Christian doctrine correctly understood is the most life-enhancing and joy-giving perspective on the face of earth.

I have promised not to reveal the wonderful surprises in *Man-alive,* but I cannot resist passing along a delightful sample of the author's interplay of ideas in characters. This incident takes place when Smith is an undergraduate at college, and in a fit of depression he goes late at night to see his favorite professor, Dr. Emerson Eames. The professor is described as a foremost philosopher, a student of Schopenhauer, an intellectual pessimist and cynic.

The scene is set after hours of pessimistic debate between Pro-fessor Eames and the student Smith.

> "Oh, hang the world!" said the sullen Smith, letting his fist fall on the table in idle despair.

> "Let's give it a bad name first," said the Professor calmly, "and then hang it. A puppy with hydrophobia would probably struggle

for life while we killed it; but if we were kind we should kill it. So an omniscient god would put us out of our pain. He would strike us dead."

"Why doesn't he strike us dead?" asked the undergraduate abstractedly, plunging his hands into his pockets.

"He's dead himself," said the philosopher; "that is where he is really enviable."

"To any one who thinks," proceeded Eames, "the pleasures of life, trivial and soon tasteless, are bribes to bring us into a torture chamber. We all see that for any thinking man mere extinction is the ... What are you doing? ... Are you mad? ... Put that thing down."

Dr. Eames had turned his tired but still talkative head over his shoulder, and had found himself looking into a small round black hole, rimmed by a six-sided circlet of steel, with a sort of spike standing up on the top.[34]

Of course, what the professor is facing is the muzzle of Innocent Smith's revolver, which the undergraduate has generously decided to use in helping to "put the puppy out of his pain."[35] There follows a highly comic scene where the man who had so disdained life itself literally runs for his life out to the balcony and onto a flying buttress high above the courtyard. It is there that Professor Eames is precariously perched, legs dangling from his academic robe, pleading to Smith that he would give anything to be allowed back into his room alive.

"Give anything!" cried Smith; "then, blast your impudence, give us a song!"

"What do you mean?" demanded the exasperated Eames, "What song?"

"A hymn, I think, would be most appropriate," answered the other gravely. "I'll let you off if you repeat after me the words—

'I thank the goodness and the grace
    That on my birth have smiled,
And perched me on this curious place
    A happy English child.' "[36]

The outcome is obvious. The very real proximity and probability

31

of death causes the former cynic to see everything in a new light and to be thankful for the very things he had scorned during the night. As the sun rises on a new day, the professor sings the pre-scribed hymn and is allowed to return to his quarters, now a man resplendent, renewed, and grateful to be alive.

And the professor's renewal inspires Innocent Smith to a new purpose as well. In Smith's own words,

> I mean to keep the remaining shots for people in the shameless state that you and I were in last night. . . . I mean to keep those bullets for pessimists—pills for pale people. And in this way I want to walk the world like a wonderful surprise—to float as idly as the thistledown, and come as silently as the sunrise; not to be expected any more than the thunderbolt, not to be recalled any more than the dying breeze. . . . I am going to hold a pistol to the head of Modern Man. But I shall not use it to kill him—only to bring him to life.[37]

I love this book. Every time I read it, I close the back cover with a smile on my face. I am sure that my joy is partly because of a vague pleasure I take in certain kinds of nonconformity, but the appeal and joy in *Manalive* runs much deeper than nonconformity. As the character Michael Moon observes, ". . . that fellow Smith. I have a fancy there's some method in his madness."[38] And there is of course a method in G. K. Chesterton's madness. The apparent madness of Innocent Smith contains the very essence of Chesterton's theology of joy.

While the actions of Innocent Smith are varied and unpredict-able, there is a consistency and meaning in his effects on others. Not atypical are the feelings of Inglewood and Moon on having followed Smith through a trapdoor out onto the roof.

> Their first feeling was that they had come out into eternity, and that eternity was very like topsy-turvydom. One definition oc-curred to one of them—that he had come out into the light of that lucid and radiant ignorance in which all beliefs had begun. The sky above them was full of mythology.[39]

Here we see Chesterton's rather clear pointers directing the reader toward the realms of "beliefs" and "mythology." We see one of a thousand hints at his theology of every person having been formed in the image of the spontaneous and joyful Creator.

Chesterton often wrote about madness, and his thoughts were forever defining the paradoxes among the popular scientific ideas of madness and the apparent madness that turns out to be the way of sanity and life. The paradox is seen in the author's comment on Innocent Smith:

> He filled every one with his own half-lunatic life; but it was not expressed in destruction, but rather in a dizzy and toppling construction.[40]

The very theme of *Manalive* is contained in those two words "toppling construction." Likewise, the theme of Chesterton's theology is the toppling of the deadening philosophies and conventions of modern industrial society; and the construction of the life-giving, freedom-granting, joy-making, Christian view of life as a moral adventure of continuous renewal.

Incidentally, this theology of joy was one of the aspects of Chesterton that so attracted the Protestant writer C. S. Lewis and later became the central concept in Lewis' autobiographical *Surprised by Joy*. And though my own background—speaking both biographically and theologically—is much more similar to that of Lewis than of Chesterton, I, too, find myself irresistibly drawn into Chesterton's playful and jolly approach to Christian doctrine and the world around us. Perhaps G. K. Chesterton is the needed antidote for a Christian upbringing too heavily laden with somber legalism and unrelenting guilt.

Near the end of *Manalive* Moses Gould, the incorrigible cynic, expresses the widely held opinion that goodness and happiness are essentially incompatible.

> "No," said Gould, with an unusual and convincing gravity, "I do not believe that being perfectly good in all respects would make a man merry."

> "Well," said Michael quietly, "will you tell me one thing? Which of us has ever tried it?"[41]

This conversation echoes what Chesterton had written in other contexts to the effect that Christianity "has not been tried and found wanting. It has been found difficult; and left untried."[42]

What is at first startling in *Manalive* is the use of apparent gunplay and desertion and burglary and polygamy as literary vehicles to show an innocent freedom and spontaneity, but of course such paradoxical surprises are merely part of Chesterton's formidable arsenal. Again without revealing the solutions to the novel's riddles, I will say simply that Chesterton resolves the situations in a way which is at once delightful and meaningful.

But what is truly unusual in modern debate is Chesterton's equation of the Christian virtues with joy. In *Manalive* G.K.C. carries us on "a wave of unreasonable happiness"[43] through the adventures of Innocent Smith into a world very different from what we have come to consider normal. Chesterton's is a mad world where men and women can choose to live their lives to the fullest extent of deliberate renewals and adventures. It is a world where we can actively seek the spontaneity and joy for which our Creator made us. It is a world where we can choose to live abundantly the Christian doctrine of the life, death, and resurrection of Jesus Christ.

In G. K. Chesterton's life and writings, there is a consistent concern and rebellion against the fact that modern society is destroying the spirit of joy in modern men and women. There is a campaign as in a war against the forces that would deprive humankind of romance, adventure, wonder, and play. There is an unrelenting argument against the false claims of the world that the way to human happiness is through wealth, fame, and power.

And finally there is a clear and rational statement as to the real source of human happiness.

> Hoary and bent I dance one hour:
>   What though I die at morn?
> There is a shout among the stars,
>   "To-night a child is born."[44]

When all is said and done, said Chesterton, it is Christian doctrine which contains the rational answer to the problems most basic to the human mind and soul. It is the doctrine of the original fall, of sin, of humility and repentance, of renewal and gratitude that contains the secret of human happiness.

Chesterton was clear in his belief that the extant modern philosophies and creeds had "missed and muddled the matter; through leaving out the ancient conception of humility and the thanks of the unworthy."[45] He was obviously correct in his assessment that the dominant creed of the 20th century would be the aggrandizement of the individual ego and the insatiable demand for more pleasures. In rejecting the Christian doctrine of humility and gratitude, modern men and women have found themselves increasingly difficult to please.

> Humility was largely meant as a restraint upon the arrogance and infinity of the appetites of man. He was always outstripping his mercies with his own newly invented needs. His very power of enjoyment destroyed half his joys. By asking for pleasure, he lost the chief pleasure; for the chief pleasure is surprise.[46]

The age in which we now live is truly the age of ego. It is an age in which popular psychologies and folk ethics are concerned with things like the "strong self-concept" and "high self-esteem" and "positive self-image" and "self-actualization" and "feeling good about oneself." And yet the truth is that in spite of our well-developed psycho-technology of enjoyment, modern men and women in general do not appear to be finding the satisfaction and enjoyment that the prescribed self-flattery was supposed to produce. In this connection, G.K.C. wrote,

> [W]hereas it has been supposed that the fullest possible enjoyment is to be found by extending our ego to infinity, the truth is that the fullest possible enjoyment is to be found by reducing our ego to zero.[47]

One of the greatest destructive heresies of our time is the self-centered assumption that we have a right to the benefits and pleasures in our lives. Chesterton wondered at

> ... the strange and staggering heresy that a human being has a right to dandelions; that in some extraordinary fashion we can demand the very pick of all the dandelions in the garden of Paradise; that we owe no thanks for them at all and need feel no wonder at them at all; and above all no wonder at being thought worthy to receive them.[48]

The age of the self has invited us to demand satisfaction, and in doing so we have blunted our ability to be grateful, to wonder, and to enjoy.

According to Chesterton, the key is indeed gratitude. In his tremendous book *Orthodoxy,* he wrote, "... the test of all happiness is gratitude."[49] And here we find a simple statement consistent with

Christian doctrine, but even more a profound insight into the workings of the human mind and soul. It is the unique Christian formula for happiness based on the traditional doctrine of the fall and original sin.

G.K.C. once quoted a friend as saying, "Well, anyhow, it must be obvious to anybody that the doctrine of the fall is the only cheerful view of human life."[50] The doctrine holds that humans were created in the image of God; that is, capable of being creative, free, spontaneous, joyful beings. But due to human choice, sin was brought into the essence of humanity, and there it has remained ever since. Upon recognizing the facts of human depravity and personal sin, humans can choose either to humble themselves before their Creator or to follow some other egocentric and self-destructive road of their own choosing.

Those who choose the road of humility, as defined and demonstrated by Jesus of Nazareth two millennia ago, enter into a new life of gratitude—gratitude for life; gratitude for sustenance; gratitude for every beauty, every pleasure, every love that God's providence sends their way. And in following that road of humility and gratitude, they wake up to find that they are happy—indeed more than happy: some call it blessed.

G. K. Chesterton was a man who laughed a great deal. Why did he laugh so much? How did he find so much in life to enjoy? Why did he take such pleasure in so many of the things and people around him? The answers lie deeper than in the economics of his life circumstances, deeper than in the sociology of his associations, deeper than in the psychology of his character; they lie in the very rock-bottom foundations of his theology of joy. For G. K. Chesterton humbled himself before his Creator, and in gratitude he found the blessed joy for which he was created. Chesterton was a man who heard God's laughter and chose to laugh along.

3

Coming of Age in Industrial England

The final quarter of the nineteenth century was one of continuing industrial expansion in England, the United States, and parts of western Europe. It was a time when steam power and machinery had revolutionized the way goods and services were produced and delivered, and rural populations had migrated to the cities to find work in the factories and offices of the new industries. It was a time as well when a successful few were able to accumulate incredible fortunes, and huge international monopolies were solidifying their grasp on the economies of the world.

It is not surprising that this same period of time contained a rise in new ideas—various theories, catchwords, slogans, notions, and creeds—which both formed and were formed by the prevailing forces of capitalist industrial growth. There were some whose ideologies served the purpose of legitimizing the emerging social patterns, and there were others whose ideologies challenged the emerging patterns.

Prominent among these popular ideas was that of evolutionary growth, as suggested by Charles Darwin in the field of biology and then expanded by William Graham Sumner and others into the social sciences as well. The English economist Herbert Spencer was credited with the phrase "survival of the fittest," which did much to set the tone for this period of time which historians have called the "Gilded Age."

One very clear implication of this Social Darwinism was that those who did succeed were, in fact, meant to succeed, because they were obviously the most fit to succeed. Another implication was an aura of inevitability—such as that historical events simply unfold by laws of nature—which served to justify whatever fate may befall the victims or losers in the great, competitive economic race.

On the other hand there were the dissenters, those who saw the human costs of industrial capitalism and who objected. A prominent ideology in this camp was the socialism that developed from the ideas of sociologist Karl Marx and his followers. Offended and angered by the gross exploitation of the working person by the capitalist captains of industry, the socialists called for a worldwide revolution by the workers. "Workers of the world, unite!" Marx wrote, proposing a communist future where there would be no private ownership of property, where the government would own and operate all aspects of the economy. In G. K. Chesterton's England the socialists tended to be of a mild, intellectual sort, who called themselves Fabian Socialists and who enjoyed the support of the famous George Bernard Shaw, Chesterton's dear friend and vigorous adversary.

But not all of the dissenters were socialists. Several of the literary stars of the day—including William Thackeray, Matthew Arnold, Thomas Carlyle, and Victor Hugo—wrote in protest of the rampant materialism and the dehumanization of the common worker. And one of G. K. Chesterton's favorites, Charles Dickens, used nearly every novel to protest the slum conditions and the maltreatment suffered by the poor at the hands of the industrialists.

This "Gilded Age" was also marked by the increasing prestige of the physical sciences and a growing popular sense that science was coming to replace religion as the final arbiter of truth and falsehood. Thomas Huxley, the famous popularizer of evolutionary science, proclaimed skepticism as the highest of virtues, and "blind faith" the unpardonable sin. The popular H. G. Wells and other apologists of science led an enthusiastic intelligensia into a general distrust of tradition and authority, and a belief that modern science would rid the world of superstition and enable human beings for the first time in history to take control of their own destiny.

In his later life Chesterton would describe this period of time:

> Socialism, in the style of Bernard Shaw and the Fabians, was a rising thing. We might almost say that agnosticism was an established church. There was a uniformity of unbelief . . . among educated people[1]

And finally there was that vague and happy term "progress." The idea of progress was broad enough and sufficiently ill-defined to make it a useful battle-cry for all manner of sloganeers. The concept certainly implied a bright future—for some it meant more factories and more commerce; for some it meant a utopian socialist state; for some it meant more science and less religion—and it therefore implied as well that whatever is the latest is the best. Progress became the industrial age's major justifying concept, in that anything done in the name of progress could hardly be questioned—except perhaps by a few ignorant traditionalists, literary romantics, and religious fanatics.

It was during this age of invention and industrial expansion, this age of scientific enthusiasm, this age of socialist idealism and proud agnosticism that the boy G. K. Chesterton came to adulthood. And as such his interior thoughts, his mental life, and later his public writings consisted in a dialogue with the major spokesmen of these forces of the age. From his forum as a career journalist, G.K.C. made his prolonged and untiring assaults against the folly and inhumanity he saw in the mainstream forces of his society.

It is so typical of G. K. Chesterton that even his own autobiography would begin on a note of meaningful satire. For it was into this thoroughly modern and futuristic milieu that Chesterton thrust the sarcastic opening remarks in his life's story:

> Bowing down in blind credulity, as is my custom, before mere authority and the tradition of the elders, superstitiously swallowing a story I could not test at the time by experiment or private judgement, I am firmly of the opinion that I was born on the 29th of May, 1874, on Campden Hill, Kensington . . . .[2]

Thus, from the beginning of his life's story, Chesterton forewarned his readers of his rejection of the popular modern ethos, while revealing the rational folly of claiming to accept nothing from authority and tradition.

Gilbert Keith Chesterton was the first son of Edward and Maria Chesterton. His father worked as a house-agent—we in the United States today would say he was in real estate—and his family has been described as being typical English middle-class liberals, both politically and theologically speaking. A younger brother, Cecil, was born five years later; there was also a little sister, who died very young.

By all accounts Gilbert Chesterton's childhood was a comfortable one with no major traumas to speak of. Some of his earliest memories are of a toy theater that his father built, in which Gilbert and Cecil would produce many plays through the years. This toy theater was to prove pivotal in Gilbert's later development of thoughts, particularly with regard to his ideas on fairy-land and sacramentalism. It appears that his father and mother were kind and solicitous, allowing their boys the freedom to grow and learn as they would.

There was a fad in Chesterton's time—as there still is today—for famous people to include in their memoirs all manner of scandalous or morbid details about their parents and childhood surroundings as a sort of psychological backdrop to explain the agonies and problems they have had to endure as adults. Predictably, Gilbert Chesterton would have none of it; in his *Autobiography* he wrote:

> I regret that I have no gloomy and savage father to offer to the public gaze as the true cause of all my tragic heritage; no pale-faced and partially poisoned mother whose suicidal instincts have cursed me with the temptations of the artistic temperament ... and that I cannot do my duty as a true modern, by cursing everybody who made me whatever I am. I am not clear about what that is; but I am pretty sure that most of it is my own fault.[3]

As in all of his writing, Chesterton adhered to his belief that each individual is responsible for his or her own decisions as well as their consequences.

But as an infant Chesterton was relatively slow to develop the standard signs of maturation. He did not talk until age three, and he did not read until age eight. He always loved fairy tales—he had them read to him regularly, and he was drawing illustrations for them even before he could read. In later childhood he would write and illustrate his own fairy tales, and some of these efforts have now been collected into a book called *The Coloured Lands*.

It is reported that when Gilbert's brother Cecil was born, the now-verbose Gilbert Chesterton stated prophetically at his brother's arrival, "Now I shall always have an audience." As Cecil grew and began to speak as well, the brothers began a lifelong dialogue that no doubt helped them both tremendously in their skills of forming and defending ideas. As one biographer put the case:

> As soon as Cecil could speak, he began to argue and the brothers'

intercourse thenceforward consisted of unending discussion. They always argued, they never quarrelled.[4]

This kind of amiable argumentation became a characteristic which G.K.C. retained throughout his adult life.

Although Gilbert Chesterton was highly imaginative and energetic in writing stories and verse on his own time, in school he was uninspired. In his classes he was known as a big, quiet boy, who never distinguished himself in any subject. He was prone to daydreaming and idling his classtime away. In the context of the contemporary debate as to "classical" versus "modern" education, G.K.C. threw his lot in with the classics—though less than wholeheartedly either way. Later he wrote, "I should always have chosen rather to idle at Greek than to idle at Chemistry."[5] And his approach to algebra was equally unenthusiastic, as reflected in his rhyme:

> Because I could not bear to make
> An algebraist cry
> I gazed with interest at X
> And never thought of Why[6]

So his teachers and schoolmates knew Gilbert Chesterton as that big, day-dreamy boy, who sat at the back of the room, sometimes smiling and muttering poetry to himself. And of course such an apparently absent-minded fellow would become the object of many schoolboy pranks. One such story bears repeating in full:

Mr. Oldershaw remembers that on one occasion on a very cold day they filled his pockets with snow on the playground. When class reassembled, the snow began to melt and pools to appear on the floor. A small boy raised his hand: "Please, Sir, I think the laboratory sink must be leaking again. The water is coming through and falling all over Chesterton."

The laboratory sink was an old offender and the master must have been short-sighted. "Chesterton," he said, "go up to Mr. _____ and ask him with my compliments to see that the trouble with the sink is put right immediately." Gilbert, with water still streaming from both pockets, obediently went upstairs, gave the message and returned without discovering what had happened.[7]

There was a prolonged period through his early school years when Gilbert remained undistinguished and unnoticed. His instructors thought him rather odd, but they considered him a nice enough fellow and certainly no troublemaker. But the day finally came when Gilbert's writing won the attention of the school masters, and he began to receive the recognition and promotions he had so long avoided. In G.K.C.'s own words:

> And certainly it was I who rejoiced in the neglect, and who asked for nothing better than to be neglected. It was, if anything, the authorities who dragged me, in my own despite, out of the comfortable and protected atmosphere of obscurity and failure. Personally, I was perfectly happy at the bottom of the class.[8]

All the while as he was idling in school, at home Gilbert was exposed to his father's formidable knowledge of English literature, to museums and galleries, to political arguments, and of course to his own historical plays which he wrote and acted. And he was still, always, drawing.

An event that proved to be an important turning point in G.K.C.'s life was the founding of the Junior Debating Club at his school. This club was founded by Gilbert and a few friends, and it existed for the purpose of debating mostly literature and political issues. The club became a grand success and in fact published its own journal for a time. It was the Junior Debating Club that brought Gilbert Chesterton out of the fog and "became to him a symbol of the ideal friendship. They were Knights of the Round Table. They were Jongleurs de Dieu. They were the Human Club. . . . They were his youth personified."[9] It was in the club that he met his lifelong friends, Lucian Oldershaw and Edmund Bentley. It was in the club that the people around him began to appreciate the depth of G.K.C.'s genius.

After graduation, his friends went off to Oxford and Cambridge, but Gilbert enrolled in art school instead. Again he did not apply himself to his schooling, and during this time endured what he described as the hardest period of his life. It was a time of his most troubling thoughts and doubts, and he reported even dabbling in the spiritualism that was popular at the time. He was as far from religion as ever.

As mentioned earlier, the Chesterton family background did not include a terribly warm and active religion. "In a purely religious sense," he wrote in his *Autobiography,* "I was brought up among people who were Unitarians and Universalists, but who were well aware that a great many people around them were becoming agnostics or even atheists."[10] And of this period of his young adulthood he wrote, "[M]y brother was frankly antireligious and I had no religion except the very haziest religiosity."[11]

Chesterton's notebook from this period revealed that he felt that he might be going mad. But out of his crisis there began to emerge a new consciousness, an awareness of a new direction. Later he wrote,

> My madness, which was considerable, was wholly within. But that madness was more and more moving in the direction of some vague and visionary revolt against the prosaic flatness of a nineteenth-century city and civilization; an imaginative impatience with the cylindrical hats and the rectangular houses . . . .[12]

Eventually G.K.C. began to realize that his madness was simply a reflection of the philosophical and ethical madness in which his entire life was immersed. He came to realize that the popular skepticism and pessimism among the intellectual sophisticates of his day were indeed a widespread madness that threatened the very spirit of modern men and women.

And then, finally, in his early twenties, Gilbert Chesterton's revolt began. In his *Autobiography* he explained,

> Yet I was not mad in any medical or physical sense; I was simply carrying the scepticism of my time as far as it would go. . . . When I had been for some time in these, the darkest depths of the contemporary pessimism, I had a strong inward impulse to revolt; to dislodge the incubus or throw off this nightmare.[13]

And throw it off he did. For here was launched the long and productive career of G. K. Chesterton, the eternal foe of all that saps the joy and life out of men and women in modern industrial society.

And here as well began the long process by which Chesterton pieced together the theories, the evidence and the logic that eventually led him to believe that orthodox Christian doctrine was the only realistic and hopeful view among the many available. His was not an immediate conversion, but a slow and painstaking effort to sort through the intellectual, scientific, and traditional claims to see which were true to reason and experience.

The beginning step was simply an ad hoc theory about existence itself:

> I invented a rudimentary and makeshift mystical theory of my own.
> It was substantially this; that even mere existence, reduced to its
> most primary limits, was extraordinary enough to be exciting.
> Anything was magnificent when compared with nothing.[14]

Chesterton referred to his position as "a sort of mystical minimum
of gratitude ...,"[15] and it indeed became a cornerstone for many
of his subsequent thoughts on philosophy and theology.

This theme of gratitude runs throughout Chesterton's writing,
both fiction and nonfiction. Much of his revolt was against a popular
pessimism derived from the philosopher Nietzsche, who questioned
the value of human life and the existence of God. It was in this early
stage of Chesterton's religious development that he wrote a poem
called "By the Babe Unborn":

> They should not hear from me a word
> Of selfishness or scorn
> If only I could find the door,
> If only I were born.[16]

Not to belabor the point here, but from the depth of his dark time
of pessimism, G.K.C. found himself overwhelmed with a sense of
the excitement, the adventure, the wonderful gift of life itself.

Meanwhile he continued to idle at the Slade School of Art, until
a friend asked him to write a few reviews for a weekly paper. What
happened next he told in his own words:

> ... that having entirely failed to learn how to draw or paint, I tossed
> off easily enough some criticisms of the weaker points of Rubens
> or the misdirected talents of Tintoretto. I had discovered the eas-
> iest of all professions; which I have pursued ever since.[17]

G .K. Chesterton found his niche as a journalist. As such he plunged
headlong into the life of London's Fleet Street with a gritty enthusiasm that has marked his writing ever since.

As a man G. K. Chesterton came to be known around London
as a provocative writer, a brilliant debater, a popular lecturer, a
controversialist, and a great lover of drink, song, and the company
of good friends. With his lifelong friend and ally, Hilaire Belloc,
Chesterton could be found regularly, roaring and arguing in the
various inns of London. It has been mentioned that G.K.C. appeared

genuinely to like everybody and everything; he very often described himself as "always perfectly happy."[18]

Perhaps again characteristically late, Gilbert Chesterton began to find himself yearning for the love of a woman. From his personal notebook there are poems which he wrote at this time, revealing a young man discovering a very special desire that called for a very specific kind of resolution. One such poem is called "Suddenly in the Midst":

> Suddenly in the midst of friends,
> Of brothers known to me more and more,
> And their secrets, histories, tastes, hero-worships,
> Schemes, love-affairs, known to me
>
> Suddenly I felt lonely.
> Felt like a child in a field
>   with no more games to play
> Because I have not a lady
>   to whom to send my thoughts at that hour
>   that she might crown my peace.[19]

And there are others like "Madonna Mia," which begins, "About Her whom I have not yet met/I wonder what she is doing/Now, at this sunset hour . . . ."[20] Happily for Gilbert Chesterton, he soon met Frances Blogg, a beautiful young woman of French descent. And during their long engagement, Gilbert was to pour his romantic instincts lavishly upon his Frances. An example is "To My Lady":

> God made you very carefully,
> He set a star apart for it,
> He stained it green and gold with fields
> And aureoled it with sunshine;
> He peopled it with kings, peoples, republics,
> And so made you, very carefully.
> All nature is God's book,
>   filled with his rough sketches for you.[21]

Gilbert Chesterton and Frances Blogg were married in 1901. An engaging account of their romance can be found in Maisie Ward's biography, *Gilbert Keith Chesterton.*[22]

As the years passed, G.K.C. continued developing his philosophical and religious views, never relinquishing his hold on the anchor of basic gratitude that he had discovered earlier. Once the fact of the joy of life and the logic of gratitude were firmly secured in his thoughts, then emerged the next obvious question: Gratitude to what or whom? Thus began the next phase of Chesterton's search for truth among the ideas around him.

While I shall leave the details of G.K. Chesterton's development of faith to be read in his superb and moving book *Orthodoxy*, I will say here that he reasoned his way through a series of arguments, trying to construct the perfect philosophy that would be adequate to all his questions and experience and logic. Along the way he discovered that "thankful to what" was nonsense, but "thankful to whom" made a great deal of sense. Further along the way he discovered the "whom" to be God and the incarnation of God to be Jesus of Nazareth. He summarized his discoveries in a poem:

> I live in an age of varied powers and knowledge,
> Of steam, science, democracy, journalism, art;
> But when my love rises like a sea,
> I have to go back to an obscure tribe
>   and a slain man
> To formulate a blessing.[23]

Even after having begun to understand the logic of Christian doctrine, Chesterton was still reticent to enter the church. There was much at stake, not the least of which may have been the man's reputation among his peers. In a time when there was a flood of movement among the intelligentsia away from religious dogmas, it could not have been entirely easy for an intelligent person to swim against the current. Chesterton wrote, "I had begun to discover that, in all that welter of inconsistent and incompatible heresies, the one and only really unpardonable heresy was orthodoxy."[24] In other words, modern freethinkers were ready to tolerate all kinds of irrational and erroneous ideas, but to them the one intolerable philosophy was Christian doctrine.

After living for some time in London, Gilbert and Frances Chesterton moved to a smaller community named Beaconsfield, which would be their home for the remainder of Gilbert's life. It was in Beaconsfield that G.K.C. developed his deep and lifelong friendship with Father O'Connor, a Roman Catholic priest who would become the inspiration for the priest-detective in Chesterton's popular "Father Brown" series. Through many long walks on the countryside and the exchange of many letters, the Chestertons enjoyed the friendship and guidance of Father O'Connor through the years.

Meanwhile in his journalistic writing Chesterton had been busy attacking the follies and inconsistencies he saw around him. He was particularly fond of exposing the illogic of the popular intellectual fads—such as materialist philosophy, evolution theory, scientific determinism, socialism, and, of course, "progress"—as well as the fertile field of corruption and stupidity in politics and government.

By 1903 Chesterton's attacks on the popular ideas of the day had become sufficiently threatening to draw a reply from Robert Blatchford, a well-known atheist and newspaper editor—in effect a challenge for G.K.C. to set forth his beliefs instead of simply attacking others. This was a challenge that Chesterton met with relish, first in the papers, then in his book *Heretics,* and finally in his most outstanding book of all, *Orthodoxy.*

G. K. Chesterton wrote literally volumes of essays, which were gathered into small books with titles like *Tremendous Trifles* and *All Is Grist.* He wrote several novels, among them *The Ball and the Cross, The Flying Inn,* and my favorite, *Manalive.* He wrote several books on other authors, such as *Robert Browning* and *William Blake* and *Charles Dickens.* He wrote poems, short stories, political tracts, travel notes, and even a short history of England. But through it all he insisted that he was and would remain a journalist.

As the years passed, G.K.C. became very fat, and his physical hugeness became the distinctive feature in popular descriptions of him. He was also notably slovenly in his dress from childhood throughout his life. He was aware that his physical appearance was to some shocking and offensive, and occasionally in his writing he made a good-natured quip about this fact. Typical is a poem he wrote with reference to his own corpulence, titled "A Wish":

> I wish I were a Girl Guide
> And looked so bright and neat
> And made my young subordinates
> Salute me in the street.
> But none have ever called me neat
> And few have thought me bright
> And the young who see me are amused
> And double up at sight.[25]

There are also enduring stories about Gilbert Chesterton's apparent "absent-mindedness" both as a child and as an adult. The story of the snowballs in his pockets was merely one in a lifelong series of such stories. But of course what his friends and acquaintances began to realize, as he grew older and his intellectual brilliance began to shine, was that his mind was not absent at all; it was more a case that it was forever occupied elsewhere.

G.K.C. himself tells in his *Autobiography* of an incident where he had gone to the neighbor to borrow a corkscrew and found himself trying to open his front door with the corkscrew, with his door key in the other hand. Another story recalls a telegram from G.K.C. to his wife in London, stating, "Am in Market Harborough. Where ought I to be?"

In all of the mundane matters of taking care of himself and his appearances, G. K. Chesterton was what would no doubt today be called a complete and utter slob. Appearances and clothing were to him simply, absolutely unimportant. After marriage his wife, Frances, took on the considerable responsibility of making Chesterton presentable before his ventures into public. It was she who invented his distinctive outfit of cape and broad-hat and walkingstick.

G. K. Chesterton's friends were many and varied, because he genuinely liked most of the people he met. Possibly his closest friend was Hilaire Belloc, with whom he shared many a raging argument at a favorite tavern. Belloc was a first-rate orator, whose education and experiences of the world surpassed those of Chesterton; his influences on Chesterton's thoughts were many. Indeed, the thoughts and arguments of Chesterton and Belloc were to become so intertwined as to compel G. B. Shaw to refer to them as one beast, the "Chesterbelloc."

It was in his verbal intercourse with Hilaire Belloc that G.K.C. worked out many of his sociological and political ideas. Belloc helped him to see that there was a third alternative to capitalism and socialism in economic theory—together they invented distributism. Belloc also helped him to clarify his thoughts on historical Christianity and the church in the world.

Another friendship that G. K. Chesterton valued through the years was that of George Bernard Shaw. While Chesterton's friendship with Belloc was based on great agreement in assumptions and principles, his friendship with Shaw grew amid their great public adversity. In retrospect G.K.C. wrote of Shaw

> But I only note this error here to emphasize the fact that my controversy with G.B.S., both logically and chronologically, is from the beginning. Since then I have argued with him on almost every subject in the world; and we have always been on opposite sides, without affectation or animosity.[26]

Chesterton and Shaw were forever combatants, and yet they had the greatest respect for one another. G.K.C. added,

> I can testify that I have never read a reply by Bernard Shaw that did not leave me in a better and not a worse temper or frame of mind; which did not seem to come out of inexhaustible fountains of fair-mindedness and intellectual geniality; which did not savour somehow of that native largeness which the philosopher attributed to the Magnanimous Man. It is necessary to disagree with him as much as I do, in order to admire him as much as I do; and I am proud of him as a foe even more than as a friend.[27]

In the year 1911, G. K. Chesterton was still writing for the *Daily News* and for the *Illustrated London News*. Over the next four years he would also produce the novels *Manalive* and *The Flying Inn*; a collection of essays called *A Miscellany of Men*; *The Wisdom of Father Brown*; *The Victorian Age in Literature*; and a small play called *Magic*. During this period Gilbert suffered considerably over the famous Marconi case, in which G.K.C.'s brother Cecil was taken to court for libel—an event which I shall describe in some detail later on. And then the dreaded World War broke out in Europe. Finally, the strain of it all became too much; Gilbert fell ill.

The illness lasted several months, consisting mostly of heart trouble with complications. Gilbert lay semiconscious under the care of nurses, while his beloved Frances hoped and prayed at his bedside. There were times when he would recognize her and engage her in short conversations, then he would fade again. At one point he began talking about joining the Roman Catholic Church, and as his health began to improve he would often recite the Apostles' Creed.

Finally Gilbert did recover, and he immediately threw himself into writing for the war effort against Germany. In 1916 Cecil Chesterton joined the English army as a private, leaving the editorship of the *New Witness* in the able hands of his brother Gilbert. Eventually Cecil would lose his life in the war, and a shaken and saddened G.K.C. would continue for a time as editor of his brother's paper.

After the war, Gilbert and Frances Chesterton traveled to Jerusalem and then to Rome, and again G.K.C. found himself drawn toward the Roman Catholic Church. It had been seven years since in his illness he had spoken of joining the church, and yet even then he held back. It was one thing to have publicly developed and defended the Christian faith on moral and philosophical grounds; but it was quite another matter to consider committing himself to membership in the church.

In his book *The Catholic Church and Conversion,* Chesterton outlined his thoughts and experiences as he moved ever so slowly toward eventual reception into the Roman Catholic Church. In these pages are some of his most combative statements regarding Protestantism, and again the Protestant reader must sift through the observations and accusations to find the insights which are valuable to all Christians.

As a Roman Catholic, G.K.C. naturally adhered to the ultramontanist doctrine of the special apostolic succession of the Roman Bishop, or the Pope, and to the primacy of church authority even over the writings of the Scriptures. Accusing Protestants of "Bible-worship," he argued the absurdity of rejecting Roman authority and yet idolizing the very book which was approved and canonized by the Roman authority.[28] To Chesterton the various Protestant denominations were not churches, but sects—mere offshoots from the true church, each with its own particular error or exaggeration of a truth. "Protestants are Catholics gone wrong;" he concluded, "That is what is really meant by saying they are Christians."[29]

Resisting the urge to argue these points and others, we may learn from Chesterton's steps toward conversion nevertheless by substituting our own conceptions of the church universal into contexts where G.K.C. was clearly speaking of the Roman Church. For Gilbert Chesterton's struggles concerning the Roman Church were not unlike the struggles of many concerning the church in whatever manifestation, denomination, or sect the context may lie.

Recalling his own experiences in life, Chesterton saw three stages of resistance through which he passed before finally committing himself to the church. The first he called "Patronizing" the church—that is, beginning to notice in a purely rational sense that many of the popular claims against the church were simply irrational or false. The second stage he called "Discovering" the church—that is, becoming aware of both the falsehood and the truths about the church, unconsciously trying to be converted. The final stage of resistance he called "Running Away" from the church—that is, having seen the truth, having felt its irresistible pull; running in fear, consciously trying not to be converted. In the end, the trap that closed around him was simply the truth.

And so Gilbert Chesterton struggled for years on end, hinting along the way as to the direction of his journey, but refusing to be pushed or hurried in his actions. As early as 1912 he had mentioned to his friend Father O'Connor that he was thinking of joining the church. At about the same time he was asked by two priests in a railway station whether the rumor was true that he was thinking of joining the church, and he answered, "It's a matter that is giving me a great deal of agony of mind, and I'd be very grateful if you would pray for me."[30]

We can never know the exact event or reasoning that finally did move G.K.C. to join the church formally in 1922, but we can find some clues in his own writing. It is my guess that the paramount motivator was Chesterton's strong sense of warfare over the minds and souls of modern men and women. At one point in his writing he referred to "the duel of the Church and the world, . . ."[31] and in a letter to his mother he wrote with reference to the church,

> I think . . . that the fight for family and the free citizen and every-
> thing decent must now be waged by one fighting form of
> Christianity.[32]

In the great war for minds and souls, Chesterton saw the church as the force fighting for human dignity, reason, and freedom.[33] It appears that G.K.C. finally decided to cast off his reticence and join the great army.

Another motivating factor was no doubt Chesterton's growing appreciation for the role of the church as teacher and guide. In his book *Orthodoxy*, he wrote that the Christian church "in its practical relation to my soul is a living teacher, not a dead one."[34] The world had deceived him, but the church had undeceived him.[35] He saw the church as the only force fighting to save modern men and women from the tyranny of their own moods and fashions. The church, he wrote, "binds men to their morality when it is not identical with their mood"[36] and " . . . is the only thing which saves a man from the degrading slavery of being a child of his age."[37]

Finally, Chesterton was very careful to point out that in joining the Christian church he was not thereby abdicating his natural intelligence and reason. On the contrary, he held that the Christian church was the true champion of reason in the 20th century. He had not really known how to think clearly, he wrote, until the church taught him how. To become a Christian "is not to leave off thinking, but to learn how to think. It is so in exactly the same sense in which to recover from palsy is not to leave off moving but to learn how to move."[38]

Chesterton had known and loved Father O'Connor for years. His dear friend Hilaire Belloc had been a Roman Catholic from the start. His brother Cecil had converted to the Roman Church before the war. And his wife Frances had been waiting patiently, neither interfering nor urging, to see what Gilbert would decide with regard to conversion. After G.K.C. had joined the church, Frances joined as well, specifically on her own volition and for her own reasons.

Meanwhile the *New Witness* had died for lack of funds, and G.K.C. wanted to find a way to start it up again. He wanted to carry on the war against corruption and monopolies that his brother Cecil had waged, and there was considerable discussion as to the nature and the title of the new paper. One idea was to call it *The Distributive Review,* but in the end he called it simply *G.K.'s Weekly.* Chesterton would serve as editor of this paper for the rest of his life.

In 1919 the Chestertons had made a tour of America, and out of that visit came the book *What I Saw in America.* This book makes particularly fascinating fare for the American reader, as it is full of Chesterton's insights on American dreams and American realities, not unlike Alexis de Tocqueville's earlier *Democracy in America.* Chesterton saw that many of the ills that plagued his native England were also threatening the United States. He yearned for Americans to recapture their original political vision and, even more importantly, for "an opening of the eyes to that greater spiritual vision that was to him the supreme opportunity of the human spirit."[39] Another American tour was arranged in 1930; both tours were very successful.

In 1932 G. K. Chesterton was asked to do a series of radio talk shows for the British Broadcasting Corporation. Again Chesterton proved to be the master. Employing the same common sense and wit that made his weekly journalism so popular, Chesterton delighted his audiences and surprised his sponsors with a series of talks that proved to be highly popular.

G. K. Chesterton had begun writing his *Autobiography* many years earlier, but he had never found the time and motivation to complete it. Finally in 1936 he finished his story. At 62 years, he was still going full tilt, overtired and overworked, warning his readers about the gathering cloud in Germany and keeping up the good fight for the freedom and dignity of all people. The spring of that year was cold and bleak, and G.K.C. fell seriously ill. On June 14, 1936, he died.

During his lifetime G. K. Chesterton wrote more than 90 published books and at least as many prefaces to other authors' books. A chronology of his writings appears below.

1900	*Greybeards at Play*
	The Wild Knight and Other Poems
1901	*The Defendant*
1902	*G. F. Watts*
	Twelve Types
1903	*Robert Browning*
1904	*The Napoleon of Notting Hill*
1905	*The Club of Queer Trades*
	Heretics
1906	*Charles Dickens*
1907	*The Man Who Was Thursday*
1908	*Orthodoxy*
	All Things Considered
1909	*George Bernard Shaw*
	The Ball and the Cross
	Tremendous Trifles
	Defence of Nonsense
1910	*What's Wrong with the World?*
	William Blake
	Alarms and Discursions
	Five Types

1911	*The Innocence of Father Brown*
	Appreciations and Criticisms of the Works of Charles Dickens
	The Ballad of the White Horse
1912	*Manalive*
	A Miscellany of Men
	Simplicity of Tolstoy
	The Victorian Age in Literature
1913	*Magic* (a play)
1914	*The Wisdom of Father Brown*
	The Flying Inn
	The Barbarism of Berlin
1915	*Poems*
	Wine, Water, and Song
	The Crimes of England
	Letters to an Old Garibaldian
1916	*A Shilling for My Thoughts*
1917	*A Short History of England*
	Utopia of Userers
1919	*Irish Impressions*
1920	*The Uses of Diversity*
	The New Jerusalem
	The Superstition of Divorce
1922	*Eugenics and Other Evils*
	The Man Who Knew Too Much
	What I Saw in America
	The Ballad of St. Barbara
	Fancies versus Fads
	St. Francis of Assisi
1924	*The End of the Roman Road*
1925	*The Everlasting Man*
	Tales of the Long Bow
	William Cobbett
	The Superstitions of the Sceptic
1926	*The Incredulity of Father Brown*
	The Outline of Sanity
	A Gleaming Cohort
	The Queen of Seven Swords
	The Catholic Church and Conversion

	Culture and the Coming Peril
	Social Reform and Birth Control
1927	*Collected Poems*
	The Return of Don Quixote
	Robert Louis Stevenson
	The Secret of Father Brown
	The Judgement of Dr. Johnson (a play)
	Gloria in Profundis (a poem)
1928	*Generally Speaking*
	Essays of Today and Yesterday Series
	Short Stories of Today and Yesterday Series
	The Sword of Wood
1929	*The Poet and the Lunatics*
	Omnibus Volume—Father Brown Stories
	Ubi Ecclesia (a poem)
	The Thing
	G.K.C. as M.C.
	The Turkey and the Turk (a play)
1930	*The Grave of Arthur* (a poem)
	Come to Think of It
	The Resurrection of Rome
	Four Faultless Felons
1931	*All is Grist*
1932	*Chaucer*
	Sidelights on New London and New York
	Christendom in Dublin
	The Surprise (a play)
1933	*All I Survey*
	St. Thomas Aquinas
	Collected Poems
	Collected Prefaces to Charles Dickens's Works
1934	*Avowals and Denials*
1935	*The Scandal of Father Brown*
	George Bernard Shaw (with *Later Phases*)

	The Well and the Shallows
1936	*As I Was Saying*

Posthumous Publications

1936	*Autobiography*
1937	*The Paradoxes of Mr. Pond*
1938	*The Coloured Lands*
1940	*The End of the Armistice*
1953	*The Surprise* (a play written in 1932)

4

Telling a Good Story

G. K. Chesterton loved a good story. He loved a good story because he felt that a good story speaks joyfully to the heart. He once referred to a particular kind of story as "those popular works of fiction which are the joy of my existence,"[1] and he could never understand the pessimistic writers who seemed to use fiction to illustrate "the pangs and disappointments of emotional life."[2] Consequently, G.K.C. loved the fiction of Robert Louis Stevenson and Charles Dickens; he hated that of Thomas Hardy.

Chesterton's own fiction reflected a variety themes, but his writing was never essentially pessimistic. Though many of his settings and images were of bleak and catastrophic circumstances, there was always a current of hope that was carried through the story by his protagonists and that tended to blossom at the end of the story. And of course such a basic hope in renewal was entirely consistent with the orthodox Christian doctrine that constituted Chesterton's philosophy of life.

There has been some argument over the years as to whether G. K. Chesterton was primarily a propagandist or an artist—whether his writings are more accurately classified as polemics for the Roman Catholic point of view or as representative English literature of the Edwardian era. But the details of this rather pointless controversy need not detain us here, for a thorough reading of Chesterton's fiction and nonfiction reveals a boisterous and jolly mixture of propaganda and artistry. Thus, it should not surprise us that G. K. Chesterton is not easy to classify.

As a career journalist, Chesterton developed most of his ideas in the nonfiction format of essays, which were published regularly in the newspapers and journals of London and later collected into small books. But he was a writer of fiction as well, and he especially loved that form of fiction that might be called the detective story or the murder mystery. There was probably nothing that spread his name more widely among the reading public than his highly popular series of short, detective stories known as the Father Brown series. He also wrote several novels, each illustrating the important themes which G.K.C. advocated throughout his life.

Though Chesterton never considered himself particularly good at writing fiction, he nevertheless preferred stories to essays and analysis. "That is because," he explained, "a story has behind it, not merely intellect which is partly mechanical, but will, which is in its essence divine."[3] Chesterton gave to the story an importance no less than that of the mark of distinction between the beasts and those very special human creatures molded in the divine image. He wrote,

> [I]n this matter of the story comes in the real supremacy of man. Of the mechanical thing we have a full knowledge. Of the living thing we have a divine ignorance; and a divine ignorance may be called the definition of romance. . . . This thing, called Fiction, then, is the main fact of our human supremacy. If you want to know what is our human kinship with Nature, with the brutes, and with the stars, you can find cartloads of big philosophical volumes to show it you. You will find our kinship with Nature in books on geology and books on metaphysics. But if you want to find our isolation and divinity, you must pick up a penny novelette.[4]

The romance of the story and the romance of human life were among Chesterton's perennial themes, which emerged in both his essays and his fiction.

The fiction that probably brought G. K. Chesterton the widest and most lasting notoriety was the series of Father Brown detective stories. These were short stories about a detective priest, who so profoundly understands the hearts of men and women that he is able to solve the crimes more effectively than the police using their standard empirical methods. For the priest gained his education from the confessional, wherein every manner of evil had been described and repented.

There is a story about how G.K.C. was inspired to create the detective priest, Father Brown. Chesterton was introduced through friends to a Roman Catholic priest named Father O'Connor, who soon became a close friend and later officially received Chesterton into the Roman Church. But soon after they had met, the two were in conversation about some sort of crime or evil, and G.K.C. found himself astonished at the depth of the clergyman's knowledge of the subject.

But what inspired the idea for Father Brown was the fact that Chesterton heard a pair of callow Cambridge undergraduates—referring to O'Connor—disparaging the cloistered life of the priest, and suggesting that it is much better to know and confront evil head-on than to live in seclusion and naivete like the priest. The irony of these young upstarts' false assumptions was not wasted on Chesterton, and the seeds were planted for the idea of Father Brown. In his *Autobiography* Chesterton wrote,

> [T]here sprang up in my mind the vague idea of making some artistic use of these comic and yet tragic cross-purposes; and constructing a comedy in which a priest should appear to know nothing and in fact know more about crime than the criminals.[5]

And the character Father Brown was born. In Father Brown, G.K.C. set out to create a character whose exterior was as plain and unremarkable as possible:

> The point of him was to appear pointless; and one might say that his conspicuous quality was not being conspicuous. His commonplace exterior was meant to contrast with his unsuspected vigilance and intelligence; and that being so, of course I made his appearance shabby and shapeless, his face round and expressionless, his manners clumsy, and so on.[6]

And thus the unremarkable Father Brown seems to bumble his way through a series of remarkable mysteries, and each time it is he after all who outwits the criminals as well as the police.

Of course there is a greater purpose here than might at first meet the eye. There is a reason why Chesterton chose a priest rather than, say, an office clerk or an omnibus driver. There is allegory in the fact that Brown's essentially religious perspective discerns the human truth and nabs the villain, while the empirical-material methods of the authorities merely come close. For Chesterton was always willing to allow that science was a marvelous tool for coming close to the truth, but, particularly with regard to understanding human beings, it could not come quite close enough.

Another essential point to the Father Brown series was to assert that the Christian point of view is indeed rational and even more useful in understanding that mystery called the human being. This

BATTLING FOR THE MODERN MIND

point is illustrated at the end of the story "The Blue Cross." After the famous French criminal Flambeau has referred to Brown as a "celibate simpleton" and has demanded that he hand over the cross, the thief finds that he has been outwitted by the priest, who knew his criminal identity all along. Here is the pivotal dialogue:

"How in blazes do you know all these horrors?" cried Flambeau.

The shadow of a smile crossed the round, simple face of his clerical opponent.

"Oh, by being a celibate simpleton, I suppose," he said. "Has it never struck you that a man who does next to nothing but hear men's real sins is not likely to be wholly unaware of human evil? But, as a matter of fact, another part of my trade, too, made me sure you weren't a priest."

"What?" asked the thief, almost gaping.

"You attacked reason," said Father Brown. "It's bad theology."[7]

Here in a paragraph is Chesterton's belief that Christian doctrine synthesizes the most realistic view of the human mind and the most reasonable view of the human will.

Chesterton's love of surprises permeates his stories, and nowhere is this fact more delightfully illustrated than in his collection called *The Club of Queer Trades*. Here are six, separate stories with unusual mysteries having even more remarkable solutions. The string of consistency that runs through the stories consists of the narrator Charles Swinburne, his eccentric but very clever friend Basil Grant, and a series of odd characters who belong to the mysterious Club of Queer Trades.

The subjects and stories vary widely, but the reader does detect certain themes that are found in virtually all of Chesterton's writing. For example, G.K.C. the antiprogressive wrote in his description of Lord Beaumont a scathing satire on the progressive notions of the English upper classes:

He has that real disadvantage which has arisen out of the modern worship of progress and novelty; and he thinks anything odd and new must be an advance. If you went to him and proposed to eat your grandmother, he would agree with you, so long as you put it on hygienic and public grounds, as a cheap alternative to cremation. So long as you progress fast enough it seems a matter of

60

indifference to him whether you are progressing to the stars or to the devil.[8]

Chesterton's objections to the progressivism of his day will be discussed in greater detail in a later chapter.

An interesting aspect of *The Club of Queer Trades* is that in each story there appears to have been a crime committed, yet in each case the alleged crime turns out to be merely an essentially harmless act by a member of the Club. It was a matter of importance to Chesterton that people should stop to ponder the nature of such concepts as crime and madness, and much of his fiction does, in fact, explore these issues. Repeatedly G.K.C.'s stories point out that that good deeds are sometimes mistaken for crimes—as they are in *The Club of Queer Trades*—and that a true sanity is sometimes mistaken for madness.

Besides the Father Brown series and other short stories, Chesterton wrote several novels as well. Though Chesterton would be the first to admit that his novels were not great in the literary sense,[9] his purpose in writing fiction was obviously not to aspire to literary eminence. His purpose was, in fact, to illuminate the intercourse of ideas, and for this reason he did not consider himself a true novelist. "In short, I could not be a novelist," he wrote in his *Autobiography*, "because I really like to see ideas or notions wrestling naked, as it were, and not dressed up in a masquerade as men and women."[10]

But despite his self-proclaimed inability to be the novelist, Chesterton loved the novel for its insight into humanity. In defining the purpose of the novel, he wrote,

> [T]he essential is that the story is not told for the sake of its naked pointedness as an anecdote, or for the sake of the irrelevant landscapes and visions that can be caught up in it, but for the sake of some study of the difference between human beings.[11]

The story and the novel are best fitted to the uniqueness of humanity and human beings, said Chesterton, and the best fiction therefore gives a picture more true of men and women than science or philosophy can give.

> People wonder why the novel is the most popular form of literature; people wonder why it is read more than books of science or books of metaphysics. The reason is very simple; it is merely that the novel is more true than they are.[12]

Thus Chesterton attributed to the novel a level of insight into human affairs unmatched by the nonfiction efforts of the scholars of humanity.

And so this man who could not be a novelist and yet loved the human story could do no other than to attempt the novel nevertheless. The resulting novels are perhaps predictably weak on characterization and strong on "naked pointedness." All of his novels are allegories; the characaters are not fully rounded personalities, but types to illustrate certain ideas—such as Christian doctrine or socialism or imperialism. The interaction and dialogues among Chesterton's characters illustrate the interplay of major ideas, and the plots of his stories tend to take whatever unlikely turns necessary for the development of his very strong themes. Consequently, his novels tend to have the aura of a dream or fantasy about them.

There are several themes that are ineludible in Chesterton's novels. One which we have noted in the novel *Manalive* is the ways in which a sense of surprise and wonder can transform the ordinary life into romantic adventure. Common to *Manalive* and to *The Flying Inn* we saw the ubiquitous Chesterton theme of madness and sanity in a world that is itself going mad. Other common G.K.C. themes are the good sense of the commoner versus the follies of the prig; the insincerity and corruption of the government and politicians; the preference of private life over public life; a belief in limited, local loyalties rather than a broad cosmopolitanism; rational tradition as opposed to progressive fashion; and a broad supernaturalism versus a narrow materialism.

Chesterton's first novel was *The Napoleon of Notting Hill*. The story is a wild, futuristic tale wherein the King of England decrees— as a cynical, private joke—that each suburb of London is an independent city-state, with its own government, its own laws, and its own army. Most of the appointed provosts of the city-states comply only reluctantly, but Provost Adam Wayne of Notting Hill embraces the idea wholeheartedly. Eventually declaring himself the Napoleon of Notting Hill, Wayne stirs up a fierce local patriotism and a formidable local army to defend his beloved neighborhood.

The central conflict comes in the form of a proposal by the business oligarchy to build a road through the Notting Hill district, which Wayne adamantly opposes. Here is the theme of modern, industrial progressivism opposed by local tradition and loyalties. In a council of the adversaries before the King, Wayne is addressed by the King:

> "You have come, my Lord, about Pump Street?"
>
> "About the city of Notting Hill," answered Wayne, proudly, "of which Pump Street is a living and rejoicing part."
>
> "Not a very large part," said Barker, contemptuously.
>
> "That which is large enough for the rich to covet," said Wayne, drawing up his head, "is large enough for the poor to defend."[13]

And thus a type emerges in Adam Wayne: the earnest, if somewhat over-serious, idealist. The King, Auberon Quin, is also a type: the cynical humorist. Barker represents the typical politician, and Buck the typical businessman.

The highly improbable events of the story are really the playing out of the motivating ideas behind the idealist, the cynic, the politician, and the businessman. There is also a very strong element of symbolism, wherein G.K.C. drew a parallel to the cause of the Boers in the South African War. In this his first novel Chesterton declared himself clearly for the local patriotism of the Boers and against the imperialism of the English in South Africa. The South African War will be discussed in some detail in a later chapter.

As the story unfolds, Barker and Buck and the provosts of the other city-states draw together in alliance against Adam Wayne of Notting Hill. Wayne, who is alone among the principals in truly believing in the King's Charter of Cities, is troubled that the people of Notting Hill are trying to build an empire, forcing their will on the people of the other city-states. His plea to his people reflects G. K. Chesterton's plea to England regarding the Boer War and the British Empire:

> Notting Hill is a nation. Why should it condescend to be a mere Empire? . . . Do you not see that it is the glory of our achievement that we have infected the other cities with the idealism of Notting Hill?[14]

England has no business building an empire, he was saying; the South African Boers have every right to their local patriotism just as England does.

And so the story ends with a great battle between the heroic but vastly outnumbered army of Notting Hill and the massive alliance of armies from the other city-states. The symbolism is not only that Adam Wayne's Notting Hill band represents the courageous Boers in South Africa, but, even more importantly, the ideals of the human spirit, of individualism, and of the dignity of every man and woman, no matter how insigificant in the eyes of the world. The imposing foe represents not only the might of the British army, but the centralizing and impersonal forces of both imperialism and socialism that were sweeping the world.

Another conflict of major ideas was addressed in Chesterton's second novel, *The Ball and the Cross*. Here G.K.C. explored the relationships among science, politics, and religion, by pitting the atheist bookseller James Turnbull against the Catholic highlander Evan MacIan. The story is again highly unlikely, as the two principals seek to fight a duel over the matter of religion, only to be interrupted and prevented repeatedly throughout the novel.

In *The Napoleon of Notting Hill* G.K.C. had introduced the theme of madness through the character of Adam Wayne, but in *The Ball and the Cross* Chesterton developed the theme much more completely. Here the author took a closer look at the meaning of madness and sanity, as well as the problem of defining each in a society that is itself going mad. The novel ends with most of the principal characters locked up in an asylum, but then with a rather apocalyptic revolt staged by the inmates.

An interesting development in *The Ball and the Cross* is the fact that MacIan and Turnbull end by calling off their duel. For in the events and dreams of the story MacIan has come to realize that the otherworldliness of his religion needs a measure of Turnbull's rationalism and social responsibility. And likewise Turnbull has come to see that his strict materialist rationalism needs to be open to the supernatural and to Christian values. Thus, the novel asserts the essential Chesterton theme that religion and reason are not dichotomous entities, but are instead meaningfully fused in the doctrines of Christianity.

Chesterton's third novel is not recommended for the beginner. *The Man Who Was Thursday: A Nightmare* was written during Chesterton's time of wrestling with the pessimistic philosophies that dominated western Europe at that time. It is again an allegorical novel, and it is one of his most difficult to understand. In his *Autobiography* G.K.C. explained the background for this novel:

I was still oppressed with the metaphysical nightmare of negations about mind and matter, with the morbid imagery of evil, with the burden of my own mysterious brain and body; but by this time I was in revolt against them; and trying to construct a healthier conception of cosmic life.[15]

In retrospect, Chesterton himself saw *The Man Who Was Thursday: A Nightmare* as an expression of his groping to escape the popular but deadening pessimistic frame of mind.

The story follows a special police detective named Gabriel Syme, who manages to get himself elected as one of the seven members of the inner circle of an international anarchist conspiracy. As anarchists these men are dedicated to the overthrow of all governments and to the destruction of the world. Syme, whose anarchist code name is Thursday, soon finds himself confronted with a series of bizarre and baffling surprises, which culminate in the wild pursuit of the great and mysterious chief anarchist, Sunday.

There are many complicated puzzles in this novel; indeed, G.K.C. himself termed it "groping and guesswork philosophy"[16] written during his self-described "period of lunacy."[17] But some of the classic Chesterton themes run like strong currents through the story. There is the trust of the common man and the distrust of the intellectuals. There is the violent rejection of the various forms of pessimism. As a member of the philosophical police explains,

We deny the snobbish English assumption that the uneducated are the dangerous criminals. We remember the Roman Emperors. We remember the great poisoning princes of the Renaissance. We say that the dangerous criminal is the educated criminal. We say that the most dangerous criminal now is the entirely lawless modern philosopher. Compared to him, burglars and bigamists are essentially moral men; my heart goes out to them. They accept the essential ideal of man; they merely seek it wrongly.[18]

Here Chesterton again attacked the widespread pessimist and skeptic rejections of moral traditions.

The Man Who Was Thursday: A Nightmare also introduces a theme that was central to Chesterton's religious views, and which I will discuss in more detail in a later chapter on elves and fairies. It is the idea that what appears to us materially is only the inferior backside of something much more real and beautiful. Gabriel Syme tries to explain this idea to his comrades:

> [T]hat has been for me the mystery of Sunday, and it is also the mystery of the world. When I see the horrible back, I am sure the noble face is but a mask. When I see the face but for an instant, I know the back is only a jest. . . . Shall I tell you the secret of the whole world? It is that we have only known the back of the world. We see everything from behind, and it looks brutal. . . . If we could only get round in front. . . .[19]

When Chesterton wrote this novel, he had reached a point of rebellion against the brutal materialism and pessimism of English intellectuals, and here we see the seeds of what he defined later as a sacramental view of life.

Chesterton's next two novels were discussed in some detail in the chapter on God's laughter. Recall that *Manalive* and *The Flying Inn* both dealt with the favorite G.K.C. themes of wonder and romance in everyday life. In *Manalive* the character Innocent Smith sweeps into the lives of a small group of bored and pessimistic people, bringing with him a new point of view, a new attitude of appreciation toward life. In *The Flying Inn,* Dalroy and Pump traverse the countryside, similarly transforming the ordinary lives with which they come in contact.

Again in *Manalive* there is the Chestertonian allegory. The trial of Innocent Smith pits Doctor Pyne and Moses Gould—representing the scientific ideal and cynical practicality—against Arthur Inglewood and Michael Moon—representing English civility and Irish realism. As the trial progresses, the reader comes to see that Smith's apparent murder, burglary, desertion, and bigamy amount to nothing more than the man's attempts to seize the romance of life—something that is opposed by the practical scientific materialist, but something that the English people are capable of understanding and defending nevertheless.

The Flying Inn contains this same theme, but this novel ventures into the realm of politics as well. Here we begin to see Chesterton's hostility toward the habits and notions of the English upper classes—the higher criticisms, the cosmopolitanism, the parliamentary corruption, and political hypocrisy. Here Chesterton seemed to be lashing out at the fads and forces which he felt were inimical to the good of common English people. This novel is full of hilarious events and boisterous drinking songs, yet it has also a melancholy undertone that paints a rather hopeless picture of the chances of political reform.

As political themes are touched in *The Flying Inn,* they are seized in Chesterton's next novel, *The Man Who Knew Too Much.* Here is a novel that reads like a catalogue of the corruptions of the English upper class. In a series of related stories, the aristocratic Horne Fisher plays the role of detective, solving each puzzle by virtue of his tired knowledge of the vices of the upper class. His young cohort, a journalist named Harold March, finds the contents of Fisher's knowledge both shocking and bewildering, thus explaining the title of the novel.

Horne Fisher is indeed an insider in the aristocratic class. "For Fisher was one of those people who are born knowing the Prime Minister," Chesterton explained. "The knowledge seemed to have no very exhilirating effect; and in his case bore some resemblance to being born tired."[20] And in another context, "His cousins and connections ramified like a labyrinth all over the governing class of Great Britain."[21] He was certainly an aristocrat, and yet he was singularly uncomfortable with the vices of his class.

The major theme of *The Man Who Knew Too Much* concerns the corruption and hypocrisy of the ruling class. In a reflective moment, Horne Fisher states the case against his own class:

> I dare say every cigar I smoke and every liqueur I drink comes directly or indirectly from the harrying of the holy places and the persecution of the poor. After all, it needs very little poking about in the past to find that hole in the wall; that great breach in the defences of English history. It lies just under the surface of a thin sheet of sham information and instruction. . . .[22]

In this novel G.K. Chesterton developed the same political themes which he often presented in his articles in *The New Witness* and later *G.K.'s Weekly.* Here is the theme of the dishonest rich and the tortured poor. Here is the theme of folly, corruption, and hypocrisy in government. And here is a new theme of the redistribution of land.

It is as if *The Flying Inn* contains Chesterton's early complaints against the rich, and *The Man Who Knew Too Much* sharpens the focus of the complaints and begins to define a solution. One begins to see hints at Chesterton's vision when his protagonist Fisher campaigns for Parliament. Fisher tells the poacher,

> I would cut up a big estate like this into small estates for everybody, even for poachers. I would do in England as they did in Ireland: buy the big men out, if possible, get them out anyhow. A man like you ought to have a little place of his own.[23]

Here is one of the seeds that would blossom into a program for social reform that G.K.C. and his friends would later call "distributism," and which I will discuss in more detail in the chapter on dragons.

Chesterton's next two novels, *Tales of the Long Bow* and *The Return of Don Quixote,* carry on the political theme of distributism, the former with an agrarian tint and the latter with an industrial tint. Both contain Chesterton's critiques of government institutions controlled by the rich, the preference for the private life of the family, and the call for a revolution in the basic structure of English politics and society.

Like *The Man Who Knew Too Much* before it, *Tales of the Long Bow* is a series of related stories, each contributing to an overall picture of Chesterton's distributist ideal. The novel tells stories of love and family life not only as allegories having political meaning, but importantly as an illustration that it is indeed the private life of the family that is central to the distributist ideal. In a typically Chestertonian bit of play, Captain Pierce tells the American millionaire,

> The best authorities believe that the Prodigal Son stayed here for some time, and the pigs—those noble and much maligned animals—gave him such excellent advice that he returned to his family.[24]

This "excellent advice" to return to the family is very germane to what distributism was all about, and the series of episodes in this novel never lose this unifying focus.

The Return of Don Quixote carries the ideas of distributism further, and this time in a more traditionally structured novel. This novel may, in fact, be one of Chesterton's better novels, because here G.K.C. not only developed his characters much more fully, but also made his allegorical political types interact in a more complicated way. The political meanings in the conclusion of the novel are not simple; nor are the solutions to the political and social problems which they represent in modern society.

The story itself follows a small group of the English upper class as they wrestle with the issues of industrial capitalism, socialism, and a movement called "syndicalism"—which turns out to be very much consistent with Chesterton's distributism. There is as usual plenty of allegory, and there are political types: Olive Ashley, the romantic idealist of the political right; John Braintree, the scientific materialist of the political left; Michael Herne, the humorless idealist of medievalism; Rosamund Severne, the practical realist; and Douglas Murrel, the equivocating liberal.

Chesterton's markedly distributist themes abound. There are the cultural chauvinism and hypocrisies of the very rich; the indictment of the cruelties of the capitalist machinery; the exposure of corruption in politics and government; and there is the anti-progressive spirit. There are pages of explanation of the rights of the working class. There is a strong sentiment that even the poor ought to enjoy the dignity of owning their homes and tools of their trade.

And again the theme of madness rings through the novel. Michael Herne is considered alternately inspired and crazy, and in the end he rides off like Don Quixote with Douglas Murrel as Sancho Panza at his side. But again G.K.C. sends one of his pointed ironies into the heart of the issue of madness. Posing as a cabdriver, Murrel manages to switch the subjects before the Lunacy Commission, causing the commission to examine the accusing doctor instead of the intended subject. Predictably, the wrongly accused doctor behaves in a most defiant and violent manner, thus supporting the fiction that he is insane. The irony contains Chesterton's critique on the madness of scientific materialism attempting to enforce by law its own definition of madness.

The novel ends by resolving the relationships among the various political types, wherein apparently opposing types are modified or corrected by one another. Thus, for instance, the marriage of Olive Ashley and John Braintree represents on one level a synthesis of romantic idealism and scientific materialism, and on another level a corrective of both her romantic fascism and his stark socialism. But the most important marriage is no doubt that of Braintree's syndicalism and Herne's medievalism, for that union reflects Chesterton's grounding of distributist ideas in the ideals and institutions of the Middle Ages.

As the next novel's title indicates, *The Poet and the Lunatics* returns to the theme of sanity and insanity, which had been an issue in nearly every one of Chesterton's earlier novels. But this later novel takes a more focused look at the definitions of sanity and lunacy through the actions and words of the protagonist Gabriel Gale. Through the episodes of the book, the poet Gale is alternately suspected of being insane or, on the other hand, the most sane character of all. It is through these surprises and twists of viewpoint that Chesterton comments on sanity and insanity in the modern world.

It is obvious that Chesterton was far from comfortable with the fact that English law provided for a person to be committed to an asylum merely by the signature of two doctors. But what seemed to be even more distressing to G.K.C. was the fact that the doctors were invariably steeped in scientific materialism and thus were ever predisposed to consider the surprising, the unusual, the romantic, and the mystical as something very close to the frontiers of insanity. That is why the doctors in the story are so committed to putting Gale in an asylum.

But Chesterton's purpose was to define insanity in another way. *The Poet and the Lunatics* asserts that it is the poetry, the romance, and the surprises in life that make for sanity; and some of the very perspectives that are widely considered "normal" are the real insanities. Early in the novel the business agent James Hurrel illustrates the peculiar monomania of the business mind. Later there is Herbert Saunders who imagines that he can control everything with his own mind. Still later there are the deadly doctors, Wolfe and Starkey, who conspire to commit Gale to an asylum. Gale's reply to these doctors contains Chesterton's main point:

> "Why, my learned friends," he went on contemptuously, "do you really suppose you are any fitter to write a report on my mind than I am on yours? You can't see any further into me than I can into you. Not half so far.... I know what is in the back of your mind ... and it's a chaos of exceptions with no rule. You could find anything abnormal, because you have no normal. You could find anybody mad."[25]

70

This is one of my favorite G.K.C. novels, not only for the entertainment in the mystery stories, but even more for Chesterton's aggressive irreverence toward those who are most aggressively irreverent. As in the case of the trick with the doctors and the Lunacy Commission in *The Return of Don Quixote,* the story here of the doctors Wolfe and Starkey clearly questions the right of scientific psychologists to declare what is normal and what is lunacy. In this connection, G. K. Chesterton anticipated a growing body of modern studies that essentially ask the same question: who says what is normal behavior, and by what right do they say so?

But I think an even more important theme developed in *The Poet and the Lunatics* is the theme of liberty and limits. Chesterton often declared in other contexts that true liberty exists only within defined limits, and here the ruminations of Gabriel Gale establish the logic of this argument. A madman has "liberated" a little yellow canary from its cage, and Gale has watched the wild birds trying to tear it to pieces. He remembers,

> Then I saw all the brown birds were trying to kill the yellow one, and that started my thoughts off as it might anybody's. Is it always kind to set a bird at liberty? What exactly is liberty? First and foremost, surely, it is the power of a thing to be itself. In some ways the yellow bird was free in the cage. It was free to be alone. It was free to sing. In the forest its feathers would be torn to pieces and its voice choked forever. Then I began to think that being oneself, which is liberty, is itself limitation. We are limited by our brains and bodies; and if we break out, we cease to be ourselves, and, perhaps, to be anything.[26]

In the story, the man who set the canary free went on to break the fishbowl to let the goldfish escape. To the poet Gabriel Gale, these were the actions of one crazed by the modern compulsion to break the limits.

> But the man who broke the bowl merely because he thought it a prison for the fish, when it was their only possible house of life—that man was already outside the world of reason, raging with a desire to be outside everything.[27]

Chesterton was referring to the same madness that gripped his Lord Ivywood in *The Flying Inn*—the madness that irrationally considers all traditions and creeds too confining, and that imagines all acts of

71

iconoclasm as liberating. It is a madness that has come to be considered "normal" in the 20th century.

The next novel, *Four Faultless Felons,* retells the stories of four people who have managed to gain very bad reputations by virtue of actions that were harmless or actually quite good. This disparity between appearances and reality is a favorite technique of Chesterton's for creating surprise in his stories. In many cases this disparity is also an allegory for Chesterton's sacramental view of life—that what we see obviously is only the faded and distorted backside of the real truth.

In *Four Faultless Felons* we find many of the favorite Chesterton topics: imperialism, revolution, agrarianism, romanticism, sanity, liberty, and repentance, to name a few. On the other hand, neither distributism nor Roman Catholicism are central issues, and there is not the kind of revolutionary call to action as in the earlier novels. It may be that the mature G. K. Chesterton was moving toward more moderate—and perhaps more realistic—views in politics and sociology as he wrote during the postwar years.

Though the four stories in this novel run along parallel tracks, they are enough different in plot and theme to render them difficult to discuss en masse. Here we will examine only the story, "The Honest Quack," as a representative sample of the great stories in this book.

The story contains the familiar character types of the painter-poet, Mr. Walter Windrush; and the young doctor-scientist, John Judson. The action and dialogue involves incessant arguments between the mystical romanticism of Windrush and the practical materialism of Judson, which appears to culminate in Judson's committing Windrush to an insane asylum. Here, of course, is the nearly ubiquitous Chesterton theme of sanity and madness replayed again with a new twist, and the author's opinion is neatly summarized in Windrush's reaction to his stay in the sanatorium:

> I am only a poor, impracticable, poetic dreamer; but I assure you
> that I am in broad daylight. In fact, I have never been out of it,
> not even when you put me in that pleasant little sanatorium for
> a day or two. I was quite happy there; and as for the lunatics, well
> I came to the conclusion that they were rather saner than my
> friends outside.[28]

72

Chesterton never tired of questioning the sanity of those who considered themselves most certifiably, scientifically sane.

Another strong element in the story is Chesterton's anti-progressive theme. Again it is Walter Windrush who represents the author's point of view. The pragmatic Dr. Judson tells the poet that he should cut down his tree and build a garage, so that he can drive to see all the woods and forests of England. Windrush replies,

> Yes, and wherever I went, I should see petrol-pumps instead of trees. That is the logical end of your progress of science and reason—and a damned illogical end to a damned unreasonable progress. Every spot of England is to be covered with petrol stations, so that people can travel about and see more petrol stations.[29]

An enduring question in all of Chesterton's fiction and nonfiction was this: progress toward what end?

A final issue which "The Honest Quack" touches again through the dialogues of Judson and Windrush is the nature of knowledge and superstition. In the beginning of the story the doctor appears to dismiss the poet's religion as mere superstitious mumbo jumbo, but in the end Judson comes to wonder how Windrush has managed to remain so tranquil and happy through his terrible ordeals. Windrush explains,

> You tell us a great deal about Evolution and the Ascent of Man. . . . You do not believe in the Garden of Eden. You do not believe in Adam and Eve. Above all, you do not believe in the Forbidden Tree. . . . But I say to you, always have in your garden a Forbidden Tree. Always have in your life something that you may not touch. This is the secret of being young and happy forever. There was never a story so true as that story you call a fable. But you will evolve and explore and eat of the tree of knowledge, and what comes of it?[30]

These issues of evolution and scientific knowledge in Chesterton's writing will be explored in detail in the following two chapters.

It is sometimes suggested that Chesterton's last novel, *The Paradoxes of Mr. Pond,* is really not a novel at all. It can be argued that this posthumously published work is better described as a collection of short stories loosely organized under a unifying concept, much like *The Club of Queer Trades* earlier. Attempts have been made to synthesize the political allegories of the stories into a kind of allegorical novel, but most critics agree that the unity of the stories is arguable. Nevertheless, *The Paradoxes of Mr. Pond* is as entertaining to read as any of Chesterton's fiction, and its flashes of insight are no less brilliant for being less well organized.

Rather than to try to deal with all of the stories in *The Paradoxes of Mr. Pond,* here we will look at one story as perhaps a typical example of the paradoxes and surprises in store for the reader. In his story called "When Doctors Agree," Chesterton's enigmatic Mr. Pond sets the stage by uttering one of his interminable paradoxes: "I did know two men who came to agree so completely that one of them naturally murdered the other. . . ."[31] There follows the usual uproar as to what Pond could possibly mean, and then the obliging Mr. Pond telling the story to explain the paradox.

The story involves the strange murder of a Mr. James Haggis, a staunch old Scottish conservative, who had opposed every major slum reform program of the popular sociologist, Dr. Campbell. Though the murder weapon was never found, the examining detective declared that the fatal wound had been made by an unidentified sharp instrument of a rather odd shape.

As the story unfolds, the reader learns that a young student named Angus, who is a Christian, comes to be locked in uninterrupted argument—for days and nights on end—with Dr. Campbell, concerning the murder of Haggins and the ethical issues pertaining thereto. Campbell argues for the skeptical pragmatism which would justify the murder on the grounds of the public good—that is, that since Haggins had been an obstacle to philanthropic reform, his murder was therefore a charitable act. Angus, on the other hand, argues from the Ten Commandments, holding simply that it is wrong to murder another person.

In the end the mystery of Haggins' death is solved in Angus' discovery that the "knife of unusual shape" was an operating tool belonging to Dr. Campbell. When Angus confronts Campbell with the discovery, the doctor readily admits his deed but justifies it as a necessary act of "social surgery." But by this time Campbell has argued so convincingly that he has converted the young Angus to his skeptical, pragmatic way of thinking. Angus replies,

Yes, I take the same view. Also, I have had the same experience. . . .

I have had daily dealings with a man I thought was doing nothing but evil. I still think you were doing evil; even though you were serving truth. You have convinced me that my beliefs were dreams; but not that dreaming is worse than waking up. You brutally broke the dreams of the humble, sneered at the weak hopes of the bereaved. You seem cruel and inhuman to me, just as Haggis seemed cruel and inhuman to you. . . . He was good to individuals, but the crowd suffered; you are good to the crowd and an individual suffered. But, after all, you also are only an individual.[32]

At this the young Angus takes the doctor's strange knife and springs upon the old man like a wildcat. And then he yells at Campbell,

Day after day, I have itched and tingled to kill you; and been held back only by the superstition you have destroyed tonight. Day after day, you have been battering down the scruples which alone defended you from death. You wise thinker; you wary reasoner; you fool! It would be better for you tonight if I still believed in God and in his Commandment against murder. . . . One thing alone protected you and kept the peace between us: that we disagreed. Now we agree, now we are at one in thought—and deed, I can do as you would do. I can do as you have done. We are at peace.[33]

And having said these things, Angus plunges Campbell's own knife into his body.

And thus Pond's paradox is explained: when the two antagonists finally come to agreement, the one murders the other. The meanings here are fairly clear. Chesterton is saying not only that the world needs Christian ethics, but that those who sneer at Christian ethics can afford to do so only because other people adhere to Christian ethics. On another level of meaning, G.K.C. is saying that both the staunch individualist—personified in Haggins—and the social philanthropist—personified in Campbell—are ultimately prone to inhumanity, unless their benevolences and systems are informed and tempered by Christian charity.

Having looked now at a representative survey of G. K. Chesterton's fictional writings, we can see that he was an author who had definite purposes in mind. Through the characters and dialogues of his fiction, G.K.C. explored and expressed the interplay of the ideas that he considered most important to the well-being and happiness of modern men and women. And from the very clear and strong themes in his fiction, we begin to piece together a mosaic picture that is Chesterton's vision of human well-being.

Restated briefly, Chesterton's fiction suggests that people are most human and most happy when their lives are filled with surprises and romance; that people would do well to stop the wheels of progress at least for long enough to ponder the destinations to which they are turning; that those who are most eager to define and institutionalize sanity may be among the most insane of all; that the common sense of common people very often contains more wisdom than the sophistries of intellectuals; that the rich and famous are particularly unfit to govern honestly and reasonably; that all people are entitled to a decent home of their own and a humane way to earn a living; that there is much more to reality and life than materialist philosophy will dare to admit; and many, many more themes as well.

G. K. Chesterton and his critics appear to agree that his fiction does not represent technically great literature. But Chesterton could surely tell a good story, and his stories are indeed the literature of a great mind engaging the great questions and problems of our time.

5

Resisting the Spell

By the final decades of the 19th century there had grown in the industrial nations of Western Europe and North America a polymorphous body of ideas that enjoyed great popularity among the middle and upper classes, and particularly among the rich, powerful, and intellectually elite. As the young man Gilbert Chesterton came to realize, the 20th century marked the palling triumph of what amounted to an ideological spell—the nearly universal acceptance of an atheistic materialism expressed in a dogmatic belief in evolutionary science, and a rather thoughtless movement away from a regard for rational authority toward a vague notion that whatever is new must be better than the old.

In the realm of philosophy and social theory, the prominent ideas were founded upon materialist philosophy, skepticism, scientific determinism, and the ethereal concept of progress. The guiding stars of the age were the German philosophers Nietzsche and Schopenhauer, the various professors of science, and the many modern "free-thinkers" and other enthusiasts of the brave new worldviews. In the realm of economics and politics, the prominent ideas were manifested in the economic determinisms of capitalism, social Darwinism, and—to a lesser extent in England and America—socialism.

Chesterton used the term materialism in a broader sense than it is popularly used today. Modern parlance tends to speak of materialism as simply the inordinate need to accumulate material objects or wealth. But Chesterton was speaking of a philosophy, an ontological point of view in which only what is material really exists. His conception of materialism was very close to what we today might call empiricism, for the essential point is that the only acceptable realities are those that can be perceived by our five senses. It is in effect the rejection of everything that is metaphysical, supernatural, or miraculous.

77

Unlike many religious opponents of materialist philosophy, G. K. Chesterton opposed the materialists on their own terms—on the grounds of rational argument. It was always an essential premise to G.K.C. that Christian doctrine was not an irrational creed to be taken on blind faith, but instead the most rational of philosophies, fully demonstrable by evidence, logic, and experience. In the end, he contended, it was materialism that could not stand up under the tests of evidence and logic.

In one of his little books of essays, *Tremendous Trifles,* appears a delightful entry called "The Wind and the Trees," in which G.K.C. outlined the heart of his attack on materialist philosophy. In typical Chesterton form the attack was offensive, as opposed to defensive, and contained various stories to illustrate his points. He told of a very small boy who was irritated at the great wind that was violently blowing the trees nearby. At last the boy said to his mother, "Well, why don't you take away the trees, and then it wouldn't wind."[1] Chesterton then explained,

> Nothing could be more intelligent or natural than this mistake. Any one looking for the first time at the trees might fancy that they were indeed vast and titanic fans, which by their mere waving agitated the air around them for miles. Nothing, I say, could be more human and excusable than the belief that it is the trees which make the wind. Indeed, the belief is so human and excusable that it is, as a matter of fact, the belief of about ninety-nine out of a hundred of the philosophers, reformers, sociologists, and politicians of the great age in which we live. My small friend was, in fact, very like the principal modern thinkers; only much nicer.[2]

Here is Chesterton's parable in which the trees stand for all visible things and the wind for the invisible. The wind, he explained, is philosophy, religion, and revolution; the trees are cities and civilizations. We can only know that the former exist because we can see what the latter do.

Chesterton pointed out the great paradox in conscious, thinking human beings trying to claim that human thoughts are only an accident of the material environment; in "free-thinking" consisting of a belief that discredits its own thought processes; in a modern, popular rejection of the old human dogma that the wind moves the trees.

The great human heresy is that the trees move the wind. When people begin to say that the material circumstances have alone created the moral circumstances, then they have prevented all possibility of serious change.[3]

In other words, materialist philosophy taken to its logical consequence leaves no basis for moral choice or responsible action, for even these are seen as mere products of material phenomena. Incidentally, this amoral, materialist line of thought was brought to its essential and frightening fruition 60 years later by the famous behaviorist B. F. Skinner in his book, *Beyond Freedom and Dignity*.

In opposition to the materialist point of view Chesterton often pointed to such nonempirical forces as patriotism, nationalism, loyalty, love, and faith, for which men and women often fight and die if need be. Indeed, the alleged "survival instincts" in biology or the pleasure-pain principles in psychology provide inadequate explanations of such very human activities as altruism and martyrdom. There is evidence all around us, argued Chesterton, of nonmaterial, nonempirical causes in human behavior.

In this regard Chesterton wrote in *The Everlasting Man* about the "realpolitik" rendition of materialist philosophy:

It is always stubbornly and stupidly repeating that men fight for material ends, without reflecting for a moment that the material ends are hardly ever material to the men who fight. In any case no man will die for practical politics, just as no man will die for pay. Nero could not hire a hundred Christians to be eaten by lions at a shilling an hour; for men will not be martyred for money.[4]

What people will fight and possibly die for is usually something very abstract and nonmaterial—perhaps "to save democracy" or "to assert the rights of freedom" or "to defend the right to worship God."

A popular idea among the many enthusiasts of science was the notion that the observable and explainable order in the universe was proof that all of existence consisted in the playing out of vast, unchanging, physical forces. G.K.C. wrote of their habit of explaining "the order in the universe by saying that all things, even the souls of men, are leaves inevitably unfolding on an utterly unconscious tree—the blind destiny of matter."[5] He argued,

All the towering materialism which dominates the modern mind rests upon one assumption; a false assumption. It is supposed that if a thing goes on repeating itself it is probably dead; a piece of clockwork. . . . It is possible that God says every morning, "Do it again" to the sun; and every evening, "Do it again" to the moon. It may not be automatic necessity that makes all daisies alike; it may be that God makes every daisy separately, but has never got tired of making them.[6]

As we shall see in our later discussion of scientific determinism, Chesterton was always ready to argue that a belief in the hand of God requires no greater leap of faith than a belief in material fate or destiny. He wrote, "In their doubt of miracles there was a faith in a fixed and godless fate; a deep and sincere faith in the incurable routine of the cosmos."[7]

Besides his powerful argument that real, living, loving, fighting, striving, believing human beings simply do not fit the scientific conception of human life as material process, Chesterton further objected to materialism on the grounds of its practical consequences. The conceptual picture of a universe operating impersonally through mechanistic laws compelled Chesterton to write of the materialist as having "a sort of insane simplicity"[8] in which he pretends to understand everything, but everything does not seem worth understanding.

And granting that the materialist view had in fact served as the philosophical and theoretical foundation for the Industrial Revolution, Chesterton again appealed to the facts:

> . . . the one, solid, staring, stupendous fact which is before all our eyes. It is the fact that we have not only seen a modern materialist civilization rise, but we have seen it fall. We have seen industrial imperialism and individualism a *practical* failure. It is no longer a question of using the modern machinery; but of cutting loose from the wreck of it.[9]

He was referring here to the high levels of unemployment, the homeless poor, the filthy slums, the dangerous working conditions, the many inhumane consequences of industrial capitalism—issues that we will examine in more detail in a later chapter.

If the ontology of the widespread modern spell was materialism, it can be said that its creed was skepticism. Indeed, there is a logical affinity between the two, for the materialist must by definition be skeptical toward idealism or any other notion that there may be more to reality than empirical phenomena. And it was this limiting nature of materialism that Chesterton took as his key point of argument. In this matter we might say that G.K.C. was launching a counterattack, because the dominant "free-thinkers" had long been attacking Christian doctrine as being both narrow-minded and outdated.

As to narrow-mindedness, Chesterton often pointed out that materialist philosophy was certainly more limiting than any religion, and that the Christian is allowed much more freedom of thought than is the materialist:

> The Christian is quite free to believe that there is a considerable amount of settled order and inevitable development in the universe. But the materialist is not allowed to admit into his spotless machine the slightest speck of spiritualism or miracle.[10]

In another context he wrote that the modern materialist skeptic "was drugged against all that was natural in the supernatural" and that "they are forbidden to believe."[11] Here is a typical Chestertonian turning-of-the-tables on the "free-thinking" accusers.

It was also a popular habit among the modern intelligentsia to boast of having moved beyond religion, of being too broad-minded to believe in a dogma. In his *Heretics,* Chesterton replied,

> Man can be defined as an animal that makes dogmas. As he piles doctrine on doctrine and conclusion on conclusion in the formation of some tremendous scheme of philosophy and religion, he is, in the only legitimate sense of which the expression is capable, becoming more and more human. When he drops one doctrine after another in a refined scepticism, when he declines to tie himself to a system, when he says that he has outgrown definitions, when he says that he disbelieves in finality, when, in his own imagination, he sits as God, holding no form of creed but contemplating all, then he is by that very process sinking slowly backwards into the vagueness of the vagrant animals and the unconsciousness of the grass. Trees have no dogmas. Turnips are singularly broad-minded.[12]

There is nothing particularly intelligent or broad-minded about disbelieving everything.

The materialist skeptic must deny the existence of anything supernatural or miraculous. Chesterton often wrote about the methods used by materialists to deny such phenomena. The first and most common is simply to deny the event altogether: "[E]ither an ordinary man need not be believed, or an extraordinary event must not be believed."[13] Another common method of dealing with the miraculous is to explain the part that can be easily explained and simply to ignore the rest. "The materialists," wrote G.K.C., "analyse the easy part, deny the hard part and go home to their tea."[14] And finally, there is the method of "explaining away" the miraculous, often by resorting to ideas more vague and farfetched than the original miracle. G.K.C. complained that this skeptical method "discredits supernatural stories that have some foundation, simply by telling natural stories that have no foundation."[15]

Chesterton gave the example of the modern skeptic confronted with the statement that Jack climbed up the beanstalk into the sky. It would be equally rational to reply that you do not think that he did, or that he may probably have done so. But the modern skeptic would more likely say something like this:

> When we consider Jack's curious and even perilous heredity, which no doubt was derived from a female greengrocer and a profligate priest, we can easily understand how the ideas of heaven and a beanstalk came to be combined in his mind. Moreover, there is little doubt that he must have met some wandering conjurer from India, who told him about the tricks of the mango plant, and how it is sent up to the sky. We can imagine these two friends, the old man and the young, wandering in the woods together at evening, looking at the red and level clouds, as on that night when the old man pointed to a small beanstalk, and told his too imaginative companion that this also might be made to scale the heavens. And then, when we remember the quite exceptional psychology of Jack, when we remember how there was in him a union of the prosaic, the love of plain vegetables, with an almost irrelevant eagerness for the unattainable, for invisibility and the void, we shall no longer wonder that it was to him especially that was sent this sweet, though merely symbolic, dream of the tree uniting earth and heaven.[16]

This bit of satire from Chesterton's pen is not as exaggerated as one might at first imagine; one needs only to read through some of the anthropological literature on myths, rituals, and comparative religions to find passages strikingly similar and farfetched.

Chesterton objected particularly to the habit among the skeptics of attacking all creeds as if creeds and rituals represented the workings of a narrow mind.

> It is the fashion to talk of men entangled in creeds and rituals, as in chains of the mind. But in fact the sceptic is hampered by invisible chains, in his most human movements, more than the lowest slave of superstition. The man who cannot lift his eyes to the sky, or bend his knee to the earth, is crippled and caught in a network of negations. It was Rosetti, I think, who said that the worst moment of the atheist was when he felt thankful and had nobody to thank.[17]

In the end, said Chesterton, the strongest modern force against a belief in the supernatural and miracles was simply the force of conformity to popular opinion. In his day—as is the case still today—the most widespread opinion was that all of the most intelligent people were materialists, and that no intelligent, rational person could possibly believe in miracles. Again Chesterton merely appealed to the facts. There are many highly intelligent people who accept the supernatural and miracles. Chesterton recounted a discussion he had with a young skeptic on this very topic:

> [H]e at length fell back upon this question, which he delivered with an honourable heat of defiance and indignation: "Well, can you tell me any man of intellect, great in science or philosophy, who accepted the miraculous?" I said, "With pleasure. Descartes, Dr. Johnson, Newton, Faraday, Newman, Gladstone, Pasteur, Browning, Brunetiere—as many more as you please." To which that quite admirable and idealistic young man made this astonishing reply—"Oh, but of course they had to say that; they were Christians." First he challenged me to find a black swan, and then he ruled out all my swans because they were black.[18]

As one explores these issues, one begins to find that closed minds can be found as frequently among the self-proclaimed "open-minded" and "liberal" as among the most dogmatic of religionists.

But the most potent manifestation of the modern spell lay clearly in the newfound mania for science, and particularly in the scientific determinism that was spreading under the banner of evolutionary theory. The shining stars in *evolutionary theory* were the English philosopher Herbert Spenser and the naturalist Charles Darwin, who borrowed Spenser's concept of "survival of the fittest" and applied it to his findings in the field of biology. The basic hypothesis of biological evolution was that life changes, or evolves, in the direction of more complex and more efficient organisms through a process of "natural selection," wherein the random mutations that prove to be most useful for survival are those which are retained, and those that do not enhance survival are weeded out in natural competition.

So long as evolution was regarded as simply a theory of a process in nature, there appeared to be little reason for objection. But as is often the case with new ideas in science, the theory of evolution attracted such enthusiastic and widespread support that it soon captured the popular mind as the only feasible and scientific explanation that could be espoused by any intelligent, modern person.

Consequently, what began like any scientific hypothesis merely as a modest proposal to explain certain phenomena rather quickly became something very similar to a creed to be applied to all aspects of life.

> But the Darwinians advanced it with so sweeping and hasty an intolerance that it is no longer a question of one scientific theory being advanced against another scientific theory. . . . It is treated as an answer; and a final and infallible answer.[19]

Thus there developed a school of thought called social Darwinism, which applied the tenets of evolutionary theory to human behavior as well. Sociologist William Graham Sumner made much of society as a living organism, with each part or person fulfilling a certain function for the whole. Soon the principals of the giant corporations, such as railroad magnate James J. Hill, were heard citing social Darwinism to justify large companies' hostile takeovers of smaller ones. There also developed popular racial theories, in which certain races were deemed more fit to survive than others.

This latter notion was developed into a particularly aggressive form by German philosopher Friedrich Nietzsche, who claimed that the only type of person who was fit to survive was the one who had the power to claim authority. Nietzsche viewed Christianity with contempt; he saw gentleness as weakness, and he described humanitarianism as the irrational protection of the unfit and spineless.

He opposed both democracy and socialism for their interest in protecting the weak.

Of course, not all evolutionists followed Nietzsche to such radical conclusions derived from "survival of the fittest." But Chesterton was always quick to point out that certain basic principles tend toward certain final consequences, and he argued from the beginning that an evolutionary theory of humanity included the seeds of tyranny. G.K.C. warned of the evolutionist's belief "that the fittest must survive, and that any one like himself must be the fittest; that the weakest must go to the wall, and that any one he could not understand must be the weakest. . . ."[20]

But the most pernicious tyranny of all is that which convinces men and women that they have no real choices. And established Darwinism grew into a belief that not only did humans evolve from apes through inexorable natural processes, but that present human life and the future of humanity were also determined by these material, evolutionary laws of nature. Such a system ruled out not only the Christian conception of the creation of man and woman as very special beings in the very image of God, but also any idea that humans possess a free will which they can exercise for good or for evil. G.K.C. observed,

> [I]t abolishes the laws which could be broken, and substitutes laws that cannot. And that is real slavery.[21]

Here is the meaning of *scientific determinism*. The popular belief was that science had discovered the laws of nature by which human life and behavior operated. In his fiction and nonfiction G.K.C. was forever holding the tenets of scientific determinism up for scrutiny. In his novel *Manalive*, Chesterton placed the doctrine in the words of one of his characters:

> "Nothing can ever alter it; it's the wheels of the universe," went on Inglewood, in a low voice: "some men are weak and some strong, and the only thing we can do is to know that we are weak. . . . That's the upshot, old fellow. We can't trust ourselves— and we can't help it."[22]

And in a nonfiction setting he wrote,

> But the machinery of this cosmic prison was something that could not be broken; for we ourselves were only a part of its machinery.

85

We were either unable to do things or we were destined to do them.[23]

A great many modern, materialist skeptics were willing to believe the evolutionary doctrine that their own very existence, their very thoughts, and their very decisions were determined by physical processes.

Against such ideas Chesterton instinctively rebelled. "Physical nature must not be made the direct object of obedience"; he asserted, "it must be enjoyed, not worshipped."[24] To G.K.C. the very meaning of humanity lay in the possession of a free moral will and the assumption of individual responsibility for one's choices of action.

> It was the Determinist who told me, at the top of his voice, that I could not be responsible at all. And as I rather like being treated as a responsible being, and not as a lunatic let out of an asylum for the day, I began to look around for some spiritual asylum that was not merely a lunatic asylum. . . . the determinist as a demagogue; shouting to a mob of millions that no man ought to be blamed for anything he did, because it was all heredity and environment. Logically, it would stop a man from saying "Thank you" to somebody for passing the mustard. For how could he be praised for passing the mustard, if he could not be blamed for not passing the mustard?[25]

Since Chesterton's day many of the concepts and the language of scientific determinism have changed, but the basic principles still flourish in the social sciences. There are still a host of theories, both psychological and sociological, which hold that human behavior results from forces beyond the control and responsibility of individual men and women.

And so Chesterton's arguments and objections are as relevant today as they were when he wrote them. To the modern scientific determinists he would still assert,

> I deny (of course) that any human thing is destined to be anything. All the absurd physical metaphors . . . are . . . but pseudo-scientific attempts to conceal from men the awful liberty of their lonely souls.[26]

To Chesterton the basis of human dignity—the very foundation of ethics that would never treat a human being as simply another creature—was that human beings were specially created and divinely endowed with a free will.

"One would imagine," he wrote, "that the really intolerable insult to human dignity would be to say that human life is not determined by human will."[27]

Paradox and irony were always in the forefront of Chesterton's thinking, and he did not miss the irony in the modern scientific determinists calling themselves "free-thinkers" and claiming to liberate humanity from the bondage of dogmas.

> [W]hen materialism leads men to complete fatalism (as it generally does), it is quite idle to pretend that it is in any sense a liberating force. It is absurd to say that you are especially advancing freedom when you only use free thought to destroy free will. The determinists come to bind, not to loose. They may well call their law the "chain" of causation. It is the worst chain that ever fettered a human being.[28]

Religious doctrines at least leave a person free to choose belief or unbelief, good or evil; determinist theories leave no room whatsoever for real choices.

A second arena of argument in which G.K.C. challenged the claims of evolutionism concerned the very nature of human beings. We have seen that the Christian conception is one of men and women as a distinctly, qualitatively different kind of animal from all the rest. G.K.C. cited all of human history itself as evidence:

> Man is an exception, whatever else he is. If he is not the image of God, then he is a disease of the dust. If it is not true that a divine being fell, then we can only say that one of the animals went entirely off its head.... His body has got too mixed up with his soul, as we see in the supreme instance of sex.[29]

A realistic look at humanity—at both its best and its worst—provides a strong argument against the notion that men and women are simply a more completely evolved kind of animal. Chesterton's arguments against this idea are developed more fully in his essential book *The Everlasting Man.*

A third point of vulnerability at which G.K.C. attacked evolutionary theory was its teleological aspect. In explaining the processes of evolutionary change, the evolutionists tended to refer to the invisible hand of Nature as selecting among the competing organisms.

As the selections were based upon a perceived final effect—that is, the characteristics which would most likely enhance survival—there was a strong implication in evolutionary arguments that there was, after all, a rather mysterious cause guiding events toward a better effect.

Chesterton pointed out that the very people who scoffed at the idea of God turned around and blithely spoke of the actions of "Mother Nature" without a moment's hesitation. In one of his essays he wrote,

> But nature selecting those that vary in the most successful direction means nothing whatsoever, except that the successful succeed. But this tautological truism is wrapped up in clouds of mythology, by the introduction of a mythical being whom even the writer regards as a myth.... All we know is that it does survive (for the moment), and then we pride ourselves on being able to repeat the mere fact that it does survive in half a hundred variegated and flowery expressions: as that it has survival value; or that it is naturally selected for survival; or that it survives because it is the fittest for survival; or that Nature's great law of the survival of the fittest sternly commands it to survive. The critics of religion used to say that its mysteries were mummeries; but these things are in the special and real sense mummeries.... [W]e know that the materialist knows that there is no such thing as a large fastidious lady, called Nature, who points a finger at a frog.[30]

Thus, the evolutionists who ridiculed the invisible hand of the Judeo-Christian God merely substituted their own version of the invisible hand in its place.

Chesterton always delighted in catching the materialists at creating their own mythology. "Having figured as ruthless realists sweeping all spiritual visions like cobwebs out of the sky," he wrote of the evolutionists, "they then became extravagant sentimentalists over some of the common or garden flowers they found growing naturally out of the earth."[31] And in another context he wrote, "And so they identified Natural Selection with Nature; with a dogmatic finality wholly inapplicable to a biological science."[32] In this way G.K.C. reminded the apologists of evolutionary theory that their science had not purged itself of mythology and dogma after all.

As a matter of fact, Chesterton fully sympathized with their sentimentalism, and he loved mythology as much as anyone did; but he insisted that the detractors of religion at least play fair and hold both sides to the same standards. In this regard he wrote,

> We are quite ready to discuss trees and giraffes in their place, without perpetual references to God. Could the materialists not so far control the rhetorical and romantic sentimentalism as to do it without perpetual reference to Nature? Shall we make a bargain; that we will for the moment leave out our theology, if they will leave out their mythology?[33]

The materialists, he argued, found it very difficult to explain the cosmos without reference to the metaphysical, the supernatural, and the miraculous, precisely because these realms happen to be a very real part of the cosmos. Even the scientific evolutionists found themselves resorting to the mythology of Mother Nature in their efforts to form a Godless explanation of the universe.

In his book *Orthodoxy* G.K.C. traced the development of his own thoughts through the popular perspectives of his day and finally to his belief in orthodox Christian doctrine. Evolutionary theory, he explained, became more untenable and unreasonable as he delved further into its claims. In the end he wrote,

> It was Huxley and Herbert Spenser and Bradlaugh who brought me back to orthodox theology. They sowed in my mind my first wild doubts of doubt. Our grandmothers were quite right when they said that Tom Paine and the freethinkers unsettled the mind. They do. They unsettled mine horribly. The rationalist made me question whether reason was of any use whatever; and when I had finished Herbert Spenser I had got as far as doubting (for the first time) whether evolution had occurred at all.[34]

Chesterton's final statement against this popular scientific determinism of the day he put in simplest form in the words of Evan MacIan, a protagonist in his novel *The Ball and the Cross*:

> I was born and bred and taught in a complete universe. The supernatural was not natural, but it was perfectly reasonable. Nay, the supernatural to me is more reasonable than the natural; for the supernatural is a direct message from God, who is reason. I was taught that some things are natural and some things divine. I mean that some things are mechanical and some divine. . . . I was told that there was a difference between the grass and a man's will; and the difference was that a man's will was special and divine. A man's free will, I heard, was supernatural.[35]

So G.K.C. asserted that not only does the supernatural exist, but it is rational—in fact, it is supremely rational, as God is rational. And men and women created specially in the image of the rational God are divinely endowed with a free will, by which they can choose their actions and bear responsibility for the consequences.

But there were other formidable aspects to this modern spell against which G. K. Chesterton argued throughout his life. Another highly popular notion—which has not diminished but has grown even more popular in the waning decades of the 20th century— was a belief in and commitment to the vague and useful idea called progress. The term itself refers to a gradual process of betterment, and when applied to human history it is the idea that humanity is slowly, step-by-step, reaching toward a better, more advanced stage.

The compatibility of the concept of progress and the theory of evolution is obvious, but it is important to notice that the notion of progress appears to fit well with almost any theory or ethical system. Thus the capitalist measures progress in terms of capital expansion and resulting profits; the Marxist measures progress in terms of popular revolutions and movement toward state ownership of the means of production; the Nietzschean measures progress in terms of the elimination of the weak and the ascendancy of the strong; and so on. Indeed, the very popularity of the term is doubtless the result of its vagueness and consequent utility to any purpose.

One cannot, of course, object to an ideologue of any stripe speaking of progress in relation to a specific standard. But the enormous fashion in Chesterton's day was for the very well-bred and best educated to speak of progress as a force in and of itself. G.K.C. referred to

> ... an entirely new notion that everything that was bad yesterday, and worse to-day, will inevitably be right to-morrow. That large and ludicrous illusion has nothing to do with the idea of men feeling their fellow-men as fellows—or even as good fellows. It was an illusion of the intellectuals, who happened to be prigs and dictated the Victorian idea of progress.[36]

It was, I think, the "inevitably" that was most galling to Chesterton. For what he saw were a lot of privileged people with no specific goals, no standards at all, talking about how the world was moving along in the right direction.

And even today we still see the arguments based on this vague idea of progress. In greater and lesser degrees of sophistication, it is still commonly argued that a trend is desirable simply because it is "catching on everywhere." Chesterton decried "the falsity and poltroonery of this eternal modern argument from what is in fashion. The question for brave men is not whether a certain thing is increasing; the question is whether we are increasing it."[37] Again it is G.K.C.'s consistent call for rational thought and individual choices of will. In other words, the popularity of an idea is irrelevant; the real question is whether I accept it or not, and why.

In our age, when democracy is erroneously perceived as the forming of private opinion by reference to public polls, Chesterton's objections are as timely as ever. He wrote,

> When the modern sociologists talk of the necessity of accommodating one's self to the trend of the time, they forget that the trend of the time at its best consists entirely of people who will not accommodate themselves to anything. At its worst it consists of many millions of frightened creatures all accommodating themselves to a trend that is not there.[38]

The important point here is the unreality of the standard. Masses of people are expected to climb aboard the juggernaut of the future, even though no one seems to have the foggiest notion as to where the thing is going.

Chesterton's first objection to the progressive craze was simply that the term "progress" was being thrown about as the guiding principle and justifying ethic for whatever happened to be the latest trend. The spell was always cast in incantations like, "Things are getting better; go with the flow." But the very people who loved to speak of things getting "better" were the first to deny that there was any such thing as a standard "best." Chesterton observed, "As enunciated to-day 'progress' is simply a comparative of which we have not settled the superlative."[39]

The demagogues of "progress" were forever belittling those who were "behind the times" or were "standing in the way of progress." And yet the desired direction of progress changed with every passing wind of fad and fashion. A rational notion of progress, argued G.K.C., would by necessity include a fixed vision as to the final, superlative point of all betterment. He explained,

91

> Progress should mean that we are always changing the world to
> suit our vision. Progress does mean (just now) that we are always
> changing the vision. It should mean that we are slow but sure in
> bringing justice and mercy among men: it does mean that we are
> very swift in doubting the desirability of justice and mercy. . . . We
> are not altering the real to suit the ideal. We are altering the ideal:
> it is easier.[40]

In other words, the idea of progress without reference to a fixed
ideal is simply absurd.

Chesterton argued further that this elusive conception of progress was actually inimical to any real change in human conditions:

> As long as the vision of heaven is always changing, the vision of
> earth will be exactly the same. No ideal will remain long enough
> to be realized, or even partly realized. The modern young man
> will never change his environment; for he will always change his
> mind.[41]

And so another paradox emerges, wherein those whose very creed
waves the banner of endless change turn out to be the very ones
who prevent any real change from being effected.

Chesterton carried his argument against the cult of progress
further by following the rational definition to its consistent consequence. If there is to be true progress for the better, there must be
a fixed idea of what is best. And though their skeptical agnosticism
kept the freethinkers of the day from admitting the connection, the
traditional terms for a fixed idea of what is best are terms like
"morals" and "creeds" and "doctrines." Consequently Chesterton
wrote,

> Nobody has any business to use the word "progress" unless he
> has a definite creed and a cast-iron code of morals. Nobody can
> be progressive without being doctrinal.[42]

And yet, it was the advocates of progress who were quick to criticize
anything resembling religious doctrine, on the grounds that religious doctrine is unproven in a rational sense. But Chesterton
argued,

> It may be thought "dogmatic," for instance, in some circles ac-
> counted progressive, to assume the perfection or improvement
> of man in another world. But it is not thought "dogmatic" to
> assume the perfection or improvement of man in this world;

though that idea of progress is quite as unproved as the idea of immortality, and from a rationalistic point of view quite as improbable.[43]

In other words, for a progressive to call a religionist "dogmatic" is a rather empty accusation.

Another implication of progressive thought with which Chesterton took issue was the vague modernist idea that events are moving along on their own and that there is no turning back."We are subconsciously dominated," he wrote, "in all departments by the notion that there is no turning back, and it is rooted in materialism and the denial of free-will."[44] There is a widespread belief even today that human events are moving inexorably forward—both for individuals and for entire peoples—and that it is somehow impossible for them to stop and go back.

We often hear truisms like, "One can't turn back the clock," but we seldom pause to realize that the truism is simply not true: We can turn back the clock. Who says we can't? Christian doctrine is in fact predicated on the proposition that we can admit our errors, go back, and start anew—the process is called repentance and renewal, and it is accomplished a million times a day all over the world. If we cannot choose to stop and go back, then we are indeed slaves to the forces around us. G. K. Chesterton was very clear in his assessment of the personal and social problems derived from our arrogant refusal to repent our mistakes. He explained,

> Now this modern refusal to undo what has been done is not only an intellectual fault; it is a moral fault also. It is not merely our mental inability to understand the mistake we have made. It is also our spiritual refusal to admit that we have made a mistake.[45]

The progressive idea that one simply cannot go back and start over is essentially a dodge, a false ideology for the purpose of avoiding responsibility for our mistakes.

In his book *Heretics* he wrote,

> We are fond of talking about "progress;" that is a dodge to avoid discussing what is good. . . . He says, "Away with your old moral formulae; I am for progress." This, logically stated, means, "Let us not settle what is good; but let us settle whether we are getting more of it."[46]

And again there was the sneering at anything traditional or old.

It has been popular throughout the 20th century simply to dismiss the ancient traditions and creeds on the entirely unsupportable grounds that they are "outdated," and that no modern person could possibly believe such things from so long ago. Chesterton argued,

> An imbecile habit has arisen in modern controversy of saying that such and such a creed can be held in one age but cannot be held in another. Some dogma, we are told, was credible in the twelfth century, but is not credible in the twentieth. You might as well say that a certain philosophy can be believed on Mondays, but cannot be believed on Tuesdays.[47]

Elsewhere G.K.C. explained that this modernist argument did not appeal to reason at all, but was an attempt to impose a sort of "mystery of superiority"[48] over the opponent, on the grounds that the modernist was especially up-to-date and in-the-know. To the rational mind, ideas, theories, creeds and doctrines stand or fall by their own merits, no matter what decade or century may have witnessed their emergence.

But the creed of progress always held anything old or traditional in low esteem and held selected modern things necessarily in high esteem. The central concept might fairly be called a fondness for newness for newness' sake. Authority is supect; tradition is rejected; limits are resisted; creeds are disbelieved. Chesterton personified the progressive ideal in his novel *The Flying Inn* by means of a conversation between Joan Brett and the furturist Lord Ivywood:

> "Joan," he said, "I would walk where no man has walked; and find something beyond tears and laughter. My road shall be my road indeed; for I will make it, like the Romans. And my adventures shall not be in the hedges and the gutters, but in the borders of the ever-advancing brain. I will think what was unthinkable until I thought it. . . . I see the breaking of barriers . . . . beyond that I see nothing." She looked at the floor for a little time and traced patterns with her parasol, like one who has really received food for thought. Then she said suddenly:
>
> "But perhaps the breaking of barriers might be the breaking of everything."
>
> The clear and colourless eyes looked at her quite steadily.
>
> "Perhaps," said Lord Ivywood.[49]

It is clear that Chesterton considered such free-floating progressivism to be irresponsible. He detected in modern thought a carelessness when it came to practical consequences, an egotistical breaking apart of old things just for the pleasure of feeling very modern and intelligent.

> The vice of the modern notion of mental progress is that it is always something concerned with the breaking of bonds, the effacing of boundaries, the casting away of dogmas. But if there is such a thing as mental growth, it must mean the growth into more and more definite convictions, into more and more dogmas.[50]

The popular notion equated mental growth with the necessary rejection of traditional ideas, but Chesterton defined mental growth as opening one's mind to all things, old and new, and then closing it again on something rational and true.

Again as in his arguments against materialism, Chesterton accused the modernists of taking the narrower view of ideas. He wrote of

> ... the narrowness of the new ideas, the limiting effect of the future. Our modern prophetic idealism is narrow because it has undergone a persistent process of elimination. We must ask for new things because we are not allowed to ask for old things.[51]

And he accused the bright young modernists of cowardice, because they so violently attacked the ancient creeds—which were unpopular anyway and therefore had very few defenders—but left the most popular modern creeds unchallenged.

> There is not really any courage at all in attacking hoary and antiquated things, any more than in offering to fight one's grandmother. The really courageous man is he who defies tyrannies young as the morning and superstitions fresh as the first flowers. The only true free-thinker is he whose intellect is as much free from the future as from the past.[52]

The essential point to Chesterton was that there is nothing particularly broadminded in rejecting the ideas of the past merely on the grounds that they are old or traditional.

As a matter of fact, G.K.C. considered progressive modernism to be not only shortsighted, but undemocratic as well. He often spoke of "the great democracy of the dead"[53], meaning the true majority of people who happen to have lived and died before we did. And in this sense a regard for tradition is simply a democratic refusal to deny the franchise to the majority of men and women from the past.

> It is obvious that tradition is only democracy extended through time. It is trusting to a consensus of common human voices rather than some isolated or arbitrary record.... Tradition may be defined as extension of the franchise. Tradition means giving votes to the most obscure of all classes, our ancestors. It is the democracy of the dead. Tradition refuses to submit to the small and arrogant oligarchy who merely happen to be walking about.[54]

And so there are answers to the progressivist and modernist claims that were popular in Chesterton's time and are even more popular today. There is something to be said against the notion that the creeds and traditions of the past have somehow been outlived and therefore relegated to irrelevance. And there is reason to look again at our own personal and corporate avoidances of repentance and renewal. For as Chesterton has reminded us, we were created specially with free wills for the purpose of making moral choices; and if those choices are to be truly free, we must be free to look toward the future and the past. "This is," said Chesterton, "... the first freedom that I claim: the freedom to restore."[55]

Having argued with the prophets of progress on rational grounds, Chesterton went on to engage them on empirical grounds as well. Not only does this progressive ideology not hold together logically, he argued, but neither does it fit the facts that are there for all to see. There was much talk of progress in science and technology solving all human problems. Chesterton observed,

> Men of the philosophic phase represented by Mr. H. G. Wells always tended to talk as if we should soon disentangle the knots of past problems merely by more science and experiment. What they did not see is that we are always tying new knots and making new tangles, actually because of science and experiment. Progress is the mother of Problems.[56]

Chesterton's point was that the question of whether science and technology produced more solutions than problems was at least debatable.

The theory of progress may be argued; but it must be proved. It

is necessary to show that certain social stages are superior to
previous social stages on their own merits; and in many cases it
may be possible to prove it. In some cases it is certainly possible
to disprove it.[57]

We cannot accept progress as an assumption, he was saying; progress
is a hypothesis which needs to be proven.

Perhaps predictably, G. K. Chesterton was accused of being a
mere reactionary, who was trying to resist the forward flow of science. But to dismiss him as such was to miss his point entirely.

Let it be noted that this is not, as is always loosely imagined, a
reaction against material science; or a regret for mechanical invention; or a depreciation of telephones or telescopes or anything
else.[58]

Chesterton had nothing against the discoveries of science and the
inventions of technology; in fact, he spoke of many of them with
the wonder of a child. What disturbed him in the growth of the
scientific ethos was the gradual diminishing of that very human sense
of wonder and the growing habit of subordinating the human individual will to scientific programs. In this connection he wrote,

There has certainly been a rush of discovery, a rapid series of
inventions; and, in one sense, the activity is marvellous and the
rapidity may well look like magic. But it has been a rapidity in
things going stale; a rush downhill to the flat and dreary world of
the prosaic; a haste of marvellous things to lose their marvellous
character; a deluge of wonders to destroy wonder. This may be
the improvement of machinery, but it cannot possibly be the improvement of man. And since it is not the improvement of man
it cannot possibly be progress.[59]

In the last half of the 19th century, the middle and upper classes
of Europe and America came under the spell of a compelling new
way of looking at the world. It was not that there was anything really
new in materialist philosophy, nor in skepticism, nor even in empirical methods in science; what was novel was the peculiar com-
bination of these perspectives into an all-embracing evolutionary
theory and a cult-like worship of the vague concept of progress.

As G. K. Chesterton lived his manhood in the early 20th century,
he could see that this evolutionary and progressive creed had
reached so deeply into the minds of modern men and women that

it was indeed very much like a sorcerer's spell—blinding rational people to its own logical inconsistencies, and obscuring from avowed empiricists even the evidences that stood against it. But even more importantly, he could see that this materialist spell had imprisoned their imaginations even to the point where they could no longer wonder at things truly wonderful.

And so G. K. Chesterton spent much of his life's effort in trying to break the spell that had captured and deadened the spirit of modern humanity and that still holds the allegiance of the vast majority who consider themselves "enlightened" and up-to-date. In one of his essays he wrote,

> I am not objecting to the statement that the science of the modern world is wonderful; I am only objecting to the modern world because it does not wonder at it.[60]

And again, there is a line from one of Chesterton's poems, which is often quoted as containing the essence of his opposition to the modern, materialist, scientific ethos. His poem "The Mystery"[61] concludes with the line

> I wonder at not wondering.

6

Jousting with the Giant

The growth of science and technology in the latter part of the 19th century was truly astonishing. In the early part of the century the world had witnessed Michael Faraday's invention of the electric dynamo and Samuel Morse's invention of the electric telegraph. Then the next 70 years brought a flood of new discoveries and inventions—including Thomas Edison's duplex telegraph and phonograph machines, Alexander Graham Bell's telephone, George Eastman's camera with roll film, and Guglielmo Marconi's wireless radio, to name a few.

In the field of industry and transportation there appeared the steam turbine, the electric generator, Rudolf Diesel's new petroleum powered engine, the internal combustion gasoline engine, Henry Ford's mass production of the Model T Ford, and finally Orville and Wilbur Wright's unveiling of a successful flying machine. In the field of medicine Louis Pasteur invented vaccinations for anthrax and rabies, and Wilhelm Roentgen demonstrated the use of the X-ray for medical diagnosis. Also as the 20th century dawned, Russian physiologist Ivan Pavlov published his famous experiments on stimulus and response in dogs, Sigmund Freud proposed his psychoanalytic theory of the unconscious, and Albert Einstein presented his theory of relativity in physics.

The practical importance of these and many other discoveries is obvious. And it is certainly no surprise that science and technology would capture the imaginations of an entire generation who had come of age during this time of marvelous inventions. The enthusiasts for science were legionary, and the prominent scientists and advocates of science came to enjoy a degree of prestige and popularity unmatched by any other class in modern society.

But as is so often the case in human affairs, the very prestige and popularity of science proved to contain the seeds of its contamination, as many of its major advocates crossed the invisible line from humble investigator to haughty professor. Soon hypotheses were preached as doctrines, and theories began to take on the trappings of creeds. And by the dawn of the 20th century there was already an entrenched intellectual elite, who appeared to regard themselves as the guardians not of simply an exceptionally fruitful investigative method, but of an entire worldview with an exclusive monopoly on the truth.

As early as 1905 G. K. Chesterton had complained of this tendency of the science professors to dispense their infallible truths:

> Men of science are beginning ... to spell truth with a capital T, beginning to talk of the creeds they imagine themselves to have destroyed, of the discoveries that their forbears made.[1]

In other words, science was rapidly becoming the unquestioned creed of modern western society, and the men of science were willingly accepting the mantle of the high priests.

This notion of science as the new religion replacing the old was not simply a farfetched reaction on Chesterton's part. The popularizers of science, such as Thomas Huxley and H. G. Wells, were deadly in their attacks against religion, and statements about science supplanting religion had become commonplace in intellectual circles. Not atypical among these attacks was Sigmund Freud's book *The Future of an Illusion.*

The illusion to which Freud referred was, of course, religion, and in his arguments he characterized religion as infantile neurosis, as unreasonable, as absurd, as ignorant, and as intellectual dishonesty. Just as Auguste Comte had earlier suggested sociology as the brave new scientific replacement for religion, Freud generously offered psychoanalysis as the future religion for enlightened moderns. And there were a host of others who—with greater or lesser subtlety and sophistication—suggested that modern science ought to and indeed would replace the archaic dogmas of the religionists.

These were the dominant events and ideas extant in G. K. Chesterton's formative years, and this widespread and firmly established ethos stood before Chesterton like a belligerent giant challenging him to enter the contest. As G.K.C. grew into the public forum of journalism, the giant continued to grow not only in size but in aggression, as the scientific attacks against religion made every appearance of winning the day.

100

As he describes in his *Autobiography* and in his masterpiece *Orthodoxy,* Chesterton had spent his youth working through in his mind the various agnosticisms that were then in vogue. But at some time during early adulthood, he came to understand the basic sense and truth in Christian doctrine, and from that time onward he threw himself into the contest for minds with all of the fighting enthusiasm of a Knight Templar.

The first point at which G. K. Chesterton launched his counter-attack against the giant scientific ethos was in pointing out that science had become the unquestioned authority on every subject imaginable. Chesterton knew enough about the basic philosophy of science to realize that such unquestioned authority is actually contradictory to the requirements of the scientific method. Thus, such unquestioning belief in the statements of science was not only irrational in the general sense, but it was unscientific in the technical sense.

Much of Chesterton's exhortation to the advocates of science was simply that they be scientific. In one essay he wrote,

> In these days we are accused of attacking science because we want it to be scientific. Surely there is not any undue disrespect to our doctor in saying that he is our doctor, not our priest, or our wife, or ourself.[2]

The complaint was that the promoters of science were forever claiming to have cast off all authority and dogma, and to have based all of their knowledge on the strictest rational-empirical methods; when in truth they were forever making unfounded, even dogmatic statements based on little but their own authority. G.K.C. wrote,

> Quackery is false science; it is everywhere apparent in cheap and popular science; and the chief mark of it is that the men who begin by boasting that they have cast away all dogmas go on to be incessantly, impudently, and quite irrationally dogmatic....

> The general rule is that nothing must be accepted on any ancient or admitted authority, but everything must be accepted on any new or nameless authority, or accepted even more eagerly on no authority at all.[3]

And Chesterton's complaint is again as relevant today as it was when he uttered it; people still tend to suspend and surrender their faculties of reason and judgment whenever someone recites the prefacing incantations: "science has proven" or "research shows." G.K.C. complained that ". . . the writer merely states, 'Recent science has shown' ... Where all these statements come from nobody knows."[4] In such cases Chesterton would merely point out that it matters very much which scientists feel they have proven the matter, exactly how they have defined and reasoned, what is their evidence, and how did they test it empirically. In other words, it is not a valid argument simply to appeal to the authority of science; one must state clearly and precisely how such a conclusion was arrived at scientifically.

But once the discoveries of science had captured the popular imagination, few had the patience for the careful methods of real science, and an easier, pseudo-science proliferated among the intelligentsia. Chesterton described the situation thus:

> But in the great days when Science was also Fashion, when the world had to bow down not only to Darwin, but to all Darwinians, when anything labelled "Specimens" or "Sections" passed without challenge, and all the camp-followers of materialism were sacred, . . . this wild romance of popular science spread wider and wider. What is odd about it is not its truth or untruth, but the unresisted smoothness with which it spread over one field after another.[5]

Much of the pseudo-science that Chesterton was talking about consisted of the plethora of authoritative and cocksure "scientific" studies of evolution and prehistoric human beings. The early anthropological literature was full of highly speculative descriptions of prehistory—typically based upon a few artifacts, bone fragments, or scratchings on a wall, and a multitude of highly biased guesses as to their meanings. But by trading on their unquestioned prestige and plenty of "pompous and pretentious polysyllables,"[6] these promoters of the "science of man" were able to convince a great many people that they knew a great deal about prehistory. Flying in the face of these pretensions, Chesterton rejoined,

> Science knows nothing whatever about pre-historic man; for the excellent reason that he is pre-historic.[7]

Though he was widely dismissed as the voice of religious unreason, Chesterton's was a consistent call to reason and common sense.

Another point of contention by which G. K. Chesterton jousted with the giant was that so much of the popular pseudo-science was at the same time pretentious and trivial. The spirit of G.K.C.'s argument is captured well in his little rhyme from "Songs of Education":

> When Science taught mankind to breathe
> A little while ago,
> Only a wise and thoughtful few
> Were really in the know.[8]

There really was in many of these early tomes of science an over-blown sense of self-importance at having enlightened the populace on all matters for the first time.

And yet the few who bothered to go to the sources and actually read the scientific reports often found them to be rather petty arguments over the finer points of esoteric little questions with only questionable relevance to anything practical or useful. Chesterton once wrote,

> Professor Higgle and Professor Haggle may argue the hind leg off a donkey, or the hundredth leg off a centipede, to settle a question that nobody can understand but themselves.[9]

And then again in another context,

> [A]s so often happens (I grieve to say) in the controversies of the very learned, a mass of the most extraordinary nonsense has been talked on both sides.[10]

And their hypotheses and arguments appeared to change with the frequency and unpredictability of the passing breeze. It was this aspect of the popular pseudo-sciences that G.K.C. was satirizing in the person of Dr. Moses Meadows, in his novel, *The Flying Inn:*

> His later idealism grew more and more materialist; and consisted of his changing hypotheses and discoveries about the healthiest foods. There is no need to detain the reader over what has been called his Oil Period; his Seaweed Period has been authoritatively expounded in Professor Nym's valuable little work; and on the events of his Glue Period it is perhaps not very generous to dwell.[11]

Concerning this Dr. Meadows, Chesterton went on to discuss how the doctor's "Mountain Milk" discovery brought him considerable wealth and had consequently turned out to be the Truth upon which the learned scientist finally settled. This was merely

G.K.C.'s fictional rendition of another lance he carried against the giant: the fact that science was invariably yet another tool in the hands of the rich and powerful. In his book, *Heretics,* he wrote,

> [A]n enormous amount of modern ingenuity is expended on finding defences for the indefensible conduct of the powerful.[12]

And in a more facetious, but no less penetrating comment

> Science in the modern world has many uses; its chief use, however, is to provide long words to cover the errors of the rich.[13]

This thesis that science and technology are used primarily by the rich at the greater expense of the poor is one that has grown in credibility and advocacy through the 20th century. In a later chapter we will discuss some of the social and political consequences of this process, as well as the efforts that G. K. Chesterton made to combat them.

But returning here to the issues of pretention and triviality, Chesterton's arguments were not merely a case of an antagonist finding fault with obscure exceptions or a few worst cases. He was looking at the meaning of the larger picture; and this larger picture was one of the vast majority of the middle and upper classes of the industrial nations accepting as unassailable truth every word that the scientific giant might utter.

And such suspension of common sense and acquiescence to even the wildest of notions Chesterton considered an important weakness in the modern mind:

> This weakness in civilization is best expressed by saying that it cares more for science than for truth. It prides itself on its "methods" more than its results; it is satisfied with precision, discipline, good communications, rather than with the sense of reality. But there are precise falsehoods as well as precise facts. . . . This is a small but exact symbol of the failure of scientific civilization. It is so satisfied in knowing it has a photograph of a man that it never asks whether it has a likeness of him.[14]

The popular scientific photograph of modern humans was of a highly developed ape, whose entire material and nonmaterial existence consisted in the inevitable unfolding of natural processes. In this photograph there was no hint or shadow of anything resembling spirit or a soul.

But Chesterton was prepared to argue that such a photograph was at best a poor likeness of the real men and women we all know in our daily lives. He appealed to both experience and reason in asking if the giant's materialist and atheist conception really caught the essence, the truth of a human being. He wrote,

> A man who has lived and loved falls down dead and the worms eat him. That is Materialism if you like. That is Atheism if you like.[15]

Of course, very few people would put the matter in quite that way, nevertheless G.K.C. has captured the essence of these positions pretty accurately. Chesterton would argue that many people, if not most, find such a description at least somewhat discomforting precisely because they really do know that something important is missing from the picture.

There had been, of course, Chesterton's previous arguments against materialism, wherein he had cited the very abstract and sometimes supernatural motives for which people are often willing to sacrifice and even die. And again in this context Chesterton appealed to actual, observable evidence which the scientific photograph was unwilling to admit.

That obvious but inadmissable evidence was sin. In the scientific giant's zeal to discard the nonempirical concept of the human soul, it had also thrown out the quite empirical reality of sin. Chesterton many times pointed out the observable realities of sin, and contrasted these with the entirely abstract and conjectural claims that sin did not exist. Nevertheless a popular notion claimed that evolutionary theory had given rout to the archaic doctrine of the human soul and sin, and again Chesterton merely asked for a reasonable explanation as to how the one had disproved the other:

> Men thought mankind wicked because they felt wicked themselves. If a man feels wicked, I cannot see why he should suddenly feel good because somebody tells him that his ancestors once had tails. Man's primary purity and innocence may have dropped off with his tail, for all anybody knows. The only thing we all know about that primary purity and innocence is that we have not got it. Nothing can be ... more comic than to set so shadowy a thing as the conjectures made by the vaguer anthropologists about primitive man against so solid a thing as the human sense of sin. By its nature the evidence of Eden is something that one cannot find.

> By its nature the evidence of sin is something that one cannot help finding.[16]

And again in a more facetious manner, he asked,

> What can people mean when they say that science has disturbed their view of sin? What sort of view of sin could they have had before science disturbed it? Did they think that it was something to eat?[17]

What G.K.C. was so sarcastically suggesting is that of *course* a materialist will deny the existence of sin, but where is the real evidence against it? The only evidence brought was an arguable theory about humans developing physiologically from apes and a rather dogmatic insistence that certain phenomena simply do not exist. Why, he wondered, should such nebulous assertions disrupt a person's very real, experiential sense of sin?

The popular rejection of the concept of sin was rooted in that vague evolutionary notion that everything is forever in a state of development and change. Not only is the human animal evolving physically, the evolutionary progressives argued, but their very thoughts are evolving toward a higher, better state. Therefore, tradition and authority are worthless, mere impediments to the inevitable improvement of the human mind.

But again Chesterton questioned the very definition of improvement. "If everything changes, including the mind of man," he asked, "how can we tell if any change is an improvement or no?"[18] In the progressive scheme, everything becomes relative to time and fashion. "The homeless scepticism of our time," wrote G.K.C., "has reached a sub-conscious feeling that morality is somehow merely a matter of human taste—an accident of psychology."[19] And when Albert Einstein presented his theory of relativity in physics, the enthusiasts of pseudoscience seized the opportunity to borrow yet another concept and claim a vague application to all areas of life.

Soon the very educated were going around pronouncing that "everything is relative," as if the very prestige and intelligence of Albert Einstein were nodding over their shoulders. No matter that Albert Einstein himself would have found such a free-floating notion incomprehensible, the mere word "relativity" became the shining halo around the formidable head of the giant. No matter that "everything is relative" is actually an absolute statement about nothing being absolute, the giant's advocates were not to be dissuaded by such technicalities.

Chesterton objected first on logical grounds. Albert Einstein had spoken of the relativity of matter with regard to velocity—something is relative to something else. But the popular notion of relativity omitted the something else and left relativity floating in the air like a grand balloon. Chesterton complained,

> But when people begin to talk about universal relativity, as if everything were as relative as everything else, so that presumably the very notion of relativity is itself relative, only relative to nobody knows what, they are simply knocking the bottom out of the world and the human brain, and leaving a bottomless abyss of bosh.[20]

This notion that "everything is relative" and that there is nothing fixed or absolute is still today the dominant ideology of those who like to think themselves very intelligent. Today we generally call this point of view *relativism.*

And so, newly crowned with the glowing notion of relativism, the giant made another thrust against the ancient creeds and doctrines of religion. Since there are so many different creeds, the giant reasoned, and each claims to be right and the others wrong, then it follows that there is no true creed. Again, Chesterton appealed to logic:

> Don't say, "There is no true creed; for each creed believes itself right and the others wrong." Probably one of the creeds is right and the others wrong. Diversity does show that most of the views must be wrong. It does not by the faintest logic show that they all must be wrong. I suppose there is no subject on which opinions differ with more desperate sincerity than about which horse will win the Derby. These are certainly solemn convictions; men risk ruin for them. The man who puts his shirt on Potosi must believe in that animal, and each of the other men putting their last garments upon other quadrupeds must believe in them quite as sincerely. They are all serious, and most of them are wrong. But one of them is right. One of the faiths is justified; one of the horses does win; not always even the dark horse which might stand for Agnosticism, but often the obvious and popular horse of Orthodoxy.... But the point here is that something comes in first. That there were many beliefs does not destroy the fact that there was one well-founded belief.[21]

Or, again he argued,

> I believe (merely upon authority) that the world is round. That
> there may be tribes who believe it to be triangular or oblong does
> not alter the fact that it is certainly some shape, and therefore not
> any other shape. Therefore I repeat, with the wail of imprecation,
> don't say that the variety of creeds prevents you from accepting
> any creed. It is an unintelligent remark.[22]

And the same arguments applied to the popular idea that the
Christian concept of sin casts a negative shadow over everything
that exists. Chesterton argued,

> The modern instinct is that if the heart of man is evil, there is
> nothing that remains good. But the older feeling was that if the
> heart of man was ever so evil—goodness remained good.[23]

In other words, good and evil are not relative terms that are defined
by fashion. As G.K.C. stated, "Right is right, even if nobody does it.
Wrong is wrong, even if everybody is wrong about it."[24] The fact
that modern optimists like to declare themselves agnostic about
good and evil has no bearing on the facts of good and evil. The
statement, "I reject your dogma," is entirely irrelevant to what happens to be the truth.

But the giant pushed its causes further by claiming that those
who say such things are unintelligent bigots and slaves to their
dogmas. The idea developed that the only objective and unbiased
judge of these matters was the relativist, and that the person who
held to any definite opinion was simply an unthinking dogmatist.
But Chesterton argued

> [I]t is manifestly most unreasonable that intelligent men should
> be divided upon the absurd modern principle of regarding every
> man who cannot make up his mind as an impartial judge, and
> regarding every clever man who can make up his mind as a servile
> fanatic.[25]

There is nothing particularly deep or insightfully incumbent in not
being able to make up one's mind; yet agnostic relativism was popularly deemed the sign of higher intelligence. On the other hand,
there is nothing particularly unenlightened in finding a given doctrine to be sensible and true to experience; yet Christians were
popularly deemed intellectual slaves. "We call a man a bigot or a

slave of dogma because he is a thinker who has thought thoroughly and to a definite end,"[26] wrote G. K. Chesterton in defense of Christian doctrine.

There was a false dichotomy that became very popular in Chesterton's time, claiming an exclusive and adverse relationship between reason and authority. This rather simple-minded perspective still runs rampant in the textbooks of history and science in our day, generally beginning with a statement something like this: "During the Middle Ages knowledge was thought to be found and transmitted through authority—particularly that of the medieval church—but in modern scientific times, this reliance upon authority was supplanted by knowledge gained through observation and reason."

Again Chesterton began his defense with an appeal to reason itself. He argued,"Modern people talk of 'Reason versus Authority'; but authority itself involves reason, or its orders would not even be understood."[27] We have seen that to G. K. Chesterton it was an important article of faith to say that orthodox Christian doctrine was the most reasonable perspective of all, and it was consequently of great importance that the giant not be allowed this sleight-of-hand equating of doctrine with mere authority.

And yet to Chesterton authority itself deserved to be defended, as it was obviously absurd for people to claim that they had purged all "mere tradition and authority" from their views. Here was the meaning of G.K.C.'s rather frequent and sarcastic remarks about his own acceptance of facts "merely upon authority." Here was the basis of his jolly accusations that the advocates of science had set themselves up as the universal authorities. And here was the foundation of his insistence that authority very often happens to be grounded in a rational and time-tested truth.

In this connection Chesterton made the rather surprising claim that real freedom can exist only within limits; that in a very practical sense, human liberty is not found in chaos and anarchy, but wherever it is granted by institutional authority. "We are never free," he wrote, "until some institution frees us, and liberty cannot exist till it is declared by authority."[28] Thus, in contrast to the popular claim that authority is the enemy of freedom, Chesterton asserted that freedom itself always depends upon rational authority for its establishment.

His argument was the same with regard to ideas. Traditional thought and authority at their best are nothing more than the accumulation of the most reasonable ideas from the past, with the intention of handing them along to subsequent generations. What was so widely derided as the dogma of unreasonable authority was nothing more than a clear and sure statement of traditional thought. Speaking of Christian doctrine and the various heresies, Chesterton wrote,

> [F]or I know very well that it is the heretical creeds that are dead, and that it is only the reasonable dogma that lives long enough to be called antiquated.[29]

Christian doctrine can be accused of many things, Chesterton held, but it cannot reasonably be accused of being unreasonable.

The Chestertonian method of defense always contained a strong element of offense, and here again G.K.C. carried his arguments back to the laps of his opponents. In reaction to the young intellectual who sneered at dogmas, he rejoined,

> I am not over-awed by a young gentleman saying that he cannot submit his intellect to dogma; because I doubt whether he has ever used his intellect enough to define dogma.[30]

The popular habit was to dismiss the religious partisan as an unthinking slave to dogma, without really stopping to examine exactly what a dogma is, where it came from, and the nature of the partisan's reasonable conclusion that it is so.

The other point at which Chesterton threw the argument back to the opposition was again to point out the many questionable and untenable things which they themselves accepted merely on authority. Recall his earlier comments about the time "when all the camp-followers of materialism were sacred . . ." and any claim remained unchallenged if it were prefaced with "research shows." His opponents seemed ready enough to doubt anything religious, but there was a uniformity of thought among them that did not appear to doubt even the wildest claims of the giant. G.K.C. commented,

> But I, for one, have found that one advantage of a man ceasing to doubt about religion is that he is much more free to doubt about everything else.[31]

In short, Chesterton asked his critics to examine themselves and to ponder their own reliance upon authority, their own acceptance of unreason, and their own enslavement to dogma.

As the giant became more aggressive in its methods, Chesterton found himself reacting against a growing movement to bring the English populace increasingly under the control of scientific management. There were the various scientific movements in education, by which certain reformers sought to usher in a new age of mental hygiene through the schools. There was the Eugenics movement, which hoped for the creation of the Superman through the scientific management of human breeding. (See G.K.C.'s *Eugenics and Other Evils* on this topic.) There was the new criminology and other efforts in sociology to remake English society using scientific principles. There was a widespread belief that science would solve all problems, and there were many who advocated making the organs of government the handmaid of science.

Chesterton was forever vigilant about new forms of tyranny, and these efforts at scientific management he found alarming. He argued,

> The thing that really is trying to tyrannise through government is Science. The thing that really does use the secular arm is Science. And the creed that really is levying tithes and capturing schools, the creed that really is enforced by fine and imprisonment, the creed that really is proclaimed not in sermons but in statutes, and spread not by pilgrims but by policemen—that creed is the great but disputed system of thought which began with Evolution and has ended in Eugenics. Materialism is really our established Church; for the Government will really help to persecute its heretics. Vaccination, in its hundred years of experiment, has been disputed almost as much as baptism in its approximate two thousand. But it seems quite natural to our politicians to enforce vaccination; and it would seem to them madness to enforce baptism.[32]

The context here was an age in which there was much agitation against the Christian church for its alleged efforts to tyrannize through government edict. Chesterton merely turned the tables and pointed to some instances of fact.

The giant also loved to recall the persecutions that had marked the history of the Christian church, and to claim that enlightened moderns would never engage in such practices. Chesterton was never one to deny the mistakes and blemishes of the church, but neither was he one to hang his head while the pot called the kettle black. He used the term "persecution" to describe the activities of the modern advocates of science against religions.

> I am not frightened of the word "persecution" when it is attributed to the churches; nor is it in the least a term of reproach that I attribute it to the men of science. It is a term of legal fact. If it means the imposition by the police of a widely disputed theory, incapable of final proof—then our priests are not now persecuting, but our doctors are. The imposition of such dogmas constitutes a State Church.... In short, they want a new kind of State Church, which shall be an Established Church of Doubt —instead of Faith.[33]

There grew in Chesterton's England an ironic situation not unlike that of the self-consciously secular culture of the United States today, in which it is acceptable and even fashionable to advocate any point of view, with the glaring exception of traditional Christian doctrine. Chesterton quipped that in times of old, only the orthodox were allowed to discuss religion, but "modern liberty means that nobody is allowed to discuss it."[34] In our age in which every kind of violence and perversion is immortalized as entertainment, and in which every perspective from evolution to witchcraft is considered essential to compulsory education, the vigilantes of enlightenment seek to exclude from public life every trace of the Judeo-Christian heritage upon which western civilization was founded.

But even in Chesterton's England, the very modern were conspicuously congratulating themselves for having thrown off the archaic encumbrance of the medieval Christian church and having ushered in the new age of light. But Chesterton presents a rather different picture, wherein the church is likened to a lamppost:

> Suppose that a great commotion arises in the street about something, let us say a lamp-post, which many influential people desire to pull down. A grey-clad monk, who is the spirit of the Middle Ages, is approached upon the matter, and begins to say, in the arid manner of the Schoolmen, "Let us first of all consider, my brethren, the value of Light. If Light be in itself good"—At this point he is somewhat excusably knocked down. All the people make a rush for the lamp-post, the lamp-post is down in ten minutes, and they go about congratulating each other on the unmedieval practicality. But as things go on they do not work out so easily. Some people have pulled the lamp-post down because they

wanted the electric light; some because they wanted old iron; some because they wanted darkness, because their deeds were evil. Some thought it not enough of a lamp-post, some too much; some acted because they wanted to smash municipal machinery; some because they wanted to smash something. And there is war in the night, no man knowing whom he strikes. So, gradually and inevitably, to-day, to-morrow, or the next day, there comes back the conviction that the monk was right after all, and that all depends on what is the philosophy of Light. Only what we might have discussed under the gas-lamp, we now must discuss in the dark.[35]

After having been besieged for a century by the giant and its followers, the Christian church stood in G. K. Chesterton's reckoning as strong as ever. And he hastened to add that it stood so by virtue of its continuing to hold the most rational and experientially valid view of human life in the vast cosmos. Chesterton deplored the handwringing attempts of the liberal theologians to reconcile Christian doctrine with the standard of empirical science; instead, he criticized science for its metaphysics and mythology, for its authoritarianism and trivial pedantry, for its unfounded relativism and hypocritical attacks on authority, and for its misguided persecution of religion and the poor.

Though the giant stood its ground and showed little sign of retreat or weakening during Chesterton's day, G.K.C. fought the battle to the end of his life and went down fighting. His summary words on the matter were neither defeatist nor apologetic—but something closer to defiance. Having pointed out that the most advanced theories in the most advanced of the physical sciences were moving away from mechanical determinisms and toward a new realm of "uncertainty principles," Chesterton concluded,

I suggest, therefore, with great respect, that it is not even now a case of having to admit that the old religion had come very near to the truths of the most modern science. It is rather a case of the most modern science having come very near to the truths of the old religion—but not quite near enough.[36]

Tilting at Dragons

The story of Saint George and the Dragon was one of G. K. Chesterton's cherished bits of English lore, and it undoubtedly fueled his imagination with regard to the role of the individual in standing against the huge and fearful forces threatening to devour all that was worth saving. During his lifetime G.K.C. pitched a series of relentless battles against the dragons which he saw threatening to destroy England and all of modern humanity. The primary threats were the dehumanizing effects of industrial capitalism and the impersonal determinisms of socialism; the subsidiary threats were the English plutocracy and corruption in the government.

The amazing explosion of technical knowledge and industrial production during the last part of the 19th century had been accompanied by various ideologies either in support of or in opposition to the flow of events as they were taking place. The proponents of industry and commerce tended to speak in terms of "progress" and "survival of the fittest" in justifying the effects of their policies, and these ideas indeed became the most popular creed among the industrial middle and upper classes in England.

During the 18th century Scottish economist Adam Smith had expounded an economic theory which came to be known as *capitalism*. Capitalism was based on the idea of private ownership and competition for profits. Citing selfishness as the basic human motivating factor, Smith felt that the greatest happiness for the greatest number of people could be found in a system of open competition among people acting in their own self-interest.

Ideally, the capitalist system would work as a balanced system among owners, workers, and consumers. The capitalist owners would supply the tools and materials. The workers would produce the goods in exchange for a fair wage. The consumers would buy the goods, giving the capitalists enough money to pay the workers, invest in the company, and earn a profit as well. Of course, the proportions among profits, wages, and prices would have very much to do with how feasibly and fairly the system would operate.

Adam Smith's capitalist theory had been enthusiastically pursued by the emerging entrepreneurs even before the Social Darwinists supplied their added ideological supports. But by 1850 it had become clear to Charles Dickens and others that some of the consequences of industrial capitalism were abhorrent. While a select few were becoming fabulously wealthy from the growth of commerce, the great majority of the masses were driven to a state of degrading poverty.

By the time G. K. Chesterton came on the scene, most of the poor had been displaced and were huddled in the cities; wretched urban slum conditions and unemployment were widespread; those who found work often had to toil under inhumane and even dangerous conditions; and the gap between the rich and poor was widening at an alarming rate. To these facts middle and upper class England wanted to turn a blind eye, but G.K.C. was determined not to let them comfortably do so.

In his journalism he wrote strongly and he wrote often of the human evils of industrial capitalism. In a description of Glasgow, an industrial city in Scotland, he wrote,

> The tall factory chimneys seemed trying to be taller than the mountain peaks; as if this landscape were full (as its history has been full) of the very madness of ambition. The wage-slavery we live in is a wicked thing.[1]

And again in another context,

> [I]f we simply ask what has been the main feature, the upshot, the final fruit of the capitalist system, there is no doubt about the answer. The special and solid result of the reign of the employers has been—unemployment.[2]

The vital issues to Chesterton were always those of human dignity and the souls of men and women. What he found most appalling in modern industrialism was the widespread attitude that human beings, called "labor," were just another resource to be uprooted, displaced, utilized, and abandoned, all for the purpose of making a few rich capitalists even richer.

This is the huge modern heresy of altering the human soul to fit its conditions, instead of altering human conditions to fit the human soul. If soap-boiling is really inconsistent with brotherhood, so much the worse for soap-boiling, not for brotherhood. . . . Certainly it would be better to do without soap rather than to do without society. Certainly, we would sacrifice all our wires, wheels, systems, specialties, physical science and frenzied finance for one half-hour of happiness such as has often come to us with comrades in a common tavern.[3]

A major theme in Chesterton's writing was the protest of "this dehumanizing way of dealing with people who do most of the practical work on which we depend, merely because they unfortunately have to do it for a wage."[4] Chesterton was like a voice crying in the wilderness, calling the people to wake up and count the human costs of their "progress."

One of Chesterton's favorite targets was the popular business ethos which had so much admiration for the millionaire and the "self-made man." Of such a single-mindedly commercial man, G.K.C. said bluntly, "It is not 'enterprise'; it is kleptomania. He is quite mad."[5] And of the commercial ethos he wrote,

I am no admirer of the complacent commercial prosperity of England in the nineteenth century. At the best it was an individualism that ended by destroying individuality; an industrialism which has done nothing except poison the very meaning of the word industry. At the worst it turned at last into a vulgar victory of sweating and swindling.[6]

Chesterton objected vigorously to a growing body of popular literature that devoted itself to the romance of business, and he lamented the fate of a society which made heroes of its "great demigods of greed."[7] He also ridiculed the feeble protestations of the industrialists who claimed to have become millionaires only reluctantly. G.K.C. wrote of the great nobles of the 19th century who became mine owners and railway directors, and all the while they "earnestly assured everybody that they did not do this from preference, but owing to a newly-discovered Economic Law."[8]

A final criticism of industrial capitalism which Chesterton made and that subsequent events would prove clearly valid was that the powerful capitalists would continue to monopolize and expand their enterprises into giant, uncontrollable, international entities. G.K.C. wrote,

The special problem to-day is that certain powers and privileges have grown so world-wide and unwieldy that they are out of the power of the moderately rich as well as of the moderately poor. They are out of the power of everybody except a few million-aires—that is, misers.[9]

Chesterton complained that the power to determine the quality of people's lives was being concentrated increasingly in the hands of a few men "with the largest of earthly fortunes and the smallest of earthly aims."[10]

As he had protested the dehumanizing influences in skepticism and scentific determinism, Chesterton also opposed the ethos of industrial capitalism for the same reason. The reason was found in the Christian doctrine of the special creation of human beings in the image of God. As such, men and women were meant also to be creative, thinking, feeling, decision-making people, whose free moral choices determine the quality of their lives. Thus Chesterton considered it nothing less than sin and heresy to subject human beings to inhuman and degrading work and living conditions and then to try to justify oneself with talk of economic laws and inevitable forces of history.

Among the English intelligentsia, possibly the most well-known critics of the capitalist economic system were the Fabian socialists. The Fabian Society began in London in 1884, drawing its ideology from the liberalism of John Stuart Mill and from the economic theory of Karl Marx. Among the brightest stars of the early Fabian movement were Sidney and Beatrice Webb, and a young Irish writer named George Bernard Shaw.

The Fabian Society endured a stormy beginning, as it tried to define itself and the limits of its activities. As it was composed almost entirely of middle-class intellectuals, its socialism took on a rather theoretical and utopian nature, confining itself to attempts at per-suasion rather than violent revolution. As time passed, the Fabian socialists talked less of revolution and more of gradual evolution of modern men and women into the desired collectivist state of mind.

Bernard Shaw and the Fabians agreed fully with G. K. Chester-ton's condemnation of the unemployment and wretched poverty wrought by unchecked capitalism. But they differed greatly as to proposed solutions. The socialists advocated government control of all important industries—particularly railways, mines, waterworks, gas, docks, markets, and transportation—and government programs to improve the welfare of the poor. They were for women's suffrage, for Irish home rule, and for reform through taxation and education.

In response to the Fabians, G. K. Chesterton defined *socialism* as "the ownership by the organ of government (whatever it is) of all things necessary to production."[11] The socialists reasoned that, since the private capitalists had demonstrated their insatiable appetites for wealth and the unconscionable exploitation of their fellow human beings, it was obvious that unchecked self-interest would not lead—as Adam Smith had claimed—to the greatest of human happiness. In fact, the capitalist system had merely given a free hand to the rich and powerful for exploiting the masses and enriching themselves. The socialists agreed with Chesterton that capitalism had failed in its promise.[12]

So the socialist solution to the problems of capitalism and the runaway greed that it had engendered was to put the means of production into the hands of the government, which as the organ of the people would control production, wages, and prices. The Fabian Socialists were essentially utopians, who, according to G.K.C., predicted a new "equal, scientific, Socialist commonwealth, owned by the State and ruled by public officers; in fact, the commonwealth of the sublime future."[13]

As sensible as such a scheme may have seemed in the abstract, in Chesterton's view it was flawed from the beginning by the mere fact that people's lives were to be organized and run by government officials. G.K.C. recalled,

> I had early begun to doubt, and later to deny, the Socialist or any other assumption that involved a complete confidence in the State.
> I think I had begun to doubt it ever since I met the statesmen.[14]

Chesterton had reason to doubt that control by government officials would be substantially less disastrous than control by the industrialists, for he already knew the sort of men who ran the government.

But his objections to socialism ran deeper than simply a distrust of government officials; there was an instinctive rejection of the very philosophical foundations of socialist theory. From its inception in the writings of Karl Marx, socialist theory was grounded in materialist philosophy. Its basis was an assumption that humans are essentially economic animals, whose actions are determined by the historical law of dialectical materialism: an inexorable process of thesis, antithesis, and synthesis.

As an idealist, a romanticist, and a Christian, G. K. Chesterton could not accept even these basic assumptions. With regard to socialist theory he wrote,

> The theory is, roughly, this: that all the important things in history are rooted in an economic motive. In short, history is a science; a science of the search for food. . . . It is putting it too feebly to say that the history of man is not only economic. Man would not have any history if he were only economic. The need for food is certainly universal, so universal that it is not even human. Cows have an economic motive, and apparently (I dare not say what ethereal delicacies may be in a cow) only an economic motive. The cow eats grass anywhere and never eats anything else. In short, the cow does fulfil the materialist theory of history: that is why the cow has no history. "A History of Cows" would be one of the simplest and briefest of standard works. But if some cows thought it wicked to eat long grass and persecuted all who did so; if the cow with the crumpled horn were worshipped by some cows and gored to death by others; if cows began to have obvious moral preferences over and above a desire for grass, then cows would begin to have a history.[15]

Thus in his inimitable and amusing way, Chesterton expressed some very important points with regard to Marxist-socialist theory. The most important was that human actions cannot be entirely explained by economic motives; that a very important difference between humans and cows is that the former do indeed often "have obvious moral preferences over and above a desire" for material gain. G.K.C. felt that materialist economics simply could not explain such Christian virtues as charity and altruism; nor could it recognize the voluntary renunciation of power, prestige, and wealth which is the foundation of Christian humility.

In the end Chesterton's objections to the Fabians' socialist utopia were the same as his objections to the other popular determinisms of his day. He did not believe the collectivist idea "that man is really happier in a hive than in a house,"[16] nor could Chesterton accept the utopian hope that modern, scientific people would find a way to perfect themselves into G. B. Shaw's kind of "Superman." Chesterton held with the realistic and optimistic Christian doctrine of a fallen humanity and salvation by the grace of God. "Only the Christian Church," he wrote, ". . . has maintained from the beginning that the danger was not in man's environment, but in man."[17]

Having protested the injustices and cruelties of the industrial capitalists, and having rejected the materialist collectivism of the Fabian socialists, Chesterton was left with the challenge to define a better way. From Chesterton's point of view, a better way must be not only realistic, but it must be consistent with the rights of human beings as created in the image of God. In collaboration with Hilaire Belloc and a group of other friends, G.K.C. spent many years working out an economic philosophy which they called *distributism*.

One of the greatest evils that Chesterton saw in the capitalist reality, as well as in the socialist dream, was the fate of common working people. The former made them wage-slaves to the capitalists; the latter would make them wage-slaves to the government. The point was not that working for pay was somehow intrinsically repugnant, but that even the lowliest worker and the unemployed poor had a God-given right to a certain level of human dignity.

Chesterton was very clear in his belief that every family had a right to a home of their own. He wrote repeatedly in defense of "the rights of property; especially the property of the poor."[18] He wrote tirelessly in his "insistence on true individualism instead of false individualism; the distribution of private property to the individual citizens and individual families."[19] He felt that the massive displacement of the agrarian peasants into the crowded hovels of the cities was among the worst crimes of the industrial age. He wrote,

> Such an apologue is literally no exaggeration of the facts of English history. The rich did literally turn the poor out of the old guest house on to the road, briefly telling them that it was the road of progress. They did literally force them into factories and the modern wage-slavery, assuring them all the time that this was the only way to wealth and civilization.[20]

To G.K.C. the crime was despicable, and the justifying lie particularly galling.

So distributism focused primarily upon opposing the trend of large landowners usurping more and more land, leaving the former tenants homeless or huddled in city apartments. G.K.C. quoted an old English rhyme in this regard:

> You prosecute the man or woman
> Who steals the goose from off the common,
> But leave the larger felon loose
> Who steals the common from the goose.[21]

Perhaps Chesterton's best summary of the distributist ideal appears in his essay "The Homelessness of Jones" in *What's Wrong with the World*:

> Nobody's real heart is in the idea of preventing a free man from owning his own farm, or an old woman from cultivating her own garden, any more than anybody's real heart was in the heartless battle of the machines. . . . The idea of private property universal but private, the idea of families free but still families, of domesticity democratic but still domestic, of one man one house—this remains the real vision and magnet of mankind.[22]

When questioned as to the feasibility of this distributist ideal, G.K.C. replied, "Whether we can give every Englishman a free home of his own or not, at least we should desire it; and he deserves it."[23]

And finally, the sentiments of the dislocated poor were captured in G.K.C.'s little drinking-song from *Greybeards at Play*:

> The people they left the land, the land,
> But they went on working hard;
> And the village green that had got mislaid
> Turned up in the squire's back-yard:
> But twenty men of us all got work
> On a bit of his motor car. . . .[24]

So distributism was wholly antisocialist, in that it considered private property to be a sacred right. Yet the distributists opposed the reality of monopoly capitalism as well as the determinist and dehumanizing ideologies that supported it. The distributist ideal was for each family to have a home of their own, for each worker to have a decent job for a fair wage, for consumer prices to reflect only modest profits, and consequently for the distribution of wealth to have a much broader range.

As Chesterton the distributist deplored the concentration of property into the hands of a few wealthy landowners, Chesterton the democrat deplored the concentration of political power into the hands of a few wealthy men. *Plutocracy*, or rule by an exclusive group of rich people, was G.K.C.'s description of the English government of his day, for he felt that it was democratic and parliamentary in name only. The real power of the government, he believed, was the will of a very small group of rich men.

As a result of government by plutocracy, Chesterton considered English society a "social madhouse, with its top-heavy rich and its tortured poor."[25] His first objection against the resident plutocracy was that it was amoral—that is, its only ruling principle was its own political survival and material success. G.K.C. wrote,

> [F]or Plutocracy has no philosophy or morals or even meaning; it can only be a material success, that is, a base success. Plutocracy can only mean the success of plutocrats in being plutocrats.[26]

And so Chesterton's picture of English society was one in which the very wealthy saw to their own interests through the organs of government, and the poor were literally powerless to do anything about the situation.

The same people who were busy enriching themselves in commerce and justifying themselves by appealing to inevitable economic laws were the very ones who sat on the front benches for both parties in Parliament. In discussing why there was so much agreement between the principals of the two political parties, G.K.C. pointed out,

> [T]he reason they agree so much ... is really that they belong to one social class; and therefore the dining life is the real life. Tory and Liberal statesmen like each other, but it is not because they are both expansive; it is because they are both exclusive.[27]

As for the needs of the common people, Chesterton wrote,

> But in modern England neither the men nor the women have any influence at all. In this primary matter, the moulding of the landscape, the creation of a mode of life, the people are utterly impotent. They stand and stare at imperial and economic processes going on, as they might stare at the Lord Mayor's Show.[28]

So a second count against the English plutocracy was that it was utterly antidemocratic. The will of the common people had no effect on the debates and decisions of Parliament. Yes, G.K.C. was willing to admit, elections were held and polls were taken; but all of the candidates and all of the choices were determined by the same few members of the plutocracy. As long as the voters were kept busy deciding upon which of the certified elite would take the chair or which side of a trivial question to support, then the government could uphold the illusion of democracy. But Chesterton claimed that in a real democracy "... The ordinary man will decide not only how he will vote, but what he is going to vote about."[29]

Again turning to the basic Christian creed for guidance, G.K.C. pointed out the irony in the popular modern prejudice against religion and traditional morality in public life:

> England is ruled by priestcraft, but not by priests. We have in this country all that has ever been alleged against the evil side of religion; the peculiar class with privileges, the sacred words that are unpronounceable; the important things known only to the few. In fact we lack nothing except the religion.[30]

And going to the basic assumptions of the English plutocracy, Chesterton wrote,

> For the whole modern world is absolutely based on the assumption ... that the rich are trustworthy. ... The whole case for Christianity is that a man who is dependent upon the luxuries of this life is a corrupt man, spiritually corrupt, politically corrupt, financially corrupt. ... Aristocracy is not an institution: aristocracy is a sin.[31]

In other words, the oligarchy of the ruling class based its legitimacy upon the myth that the rich and famous were somehow more fit to govern; Christianity, on the other hand, bases its objection on the fact that all people are basically flawed and prone to corruption. In this regard Chesterton further explained,

> Carlyle said that men were mostly fools. Christianity, with a surer and more reverent realism, says that they are all fools. This doctrine is sometimes called the doctrine of original sin. It may also be described as the doctrine of the equality of men.[32]

So here is Christian doctrine as the great leveler, "the only thing left that has any real right to question the power of the well-nurtured or the well-bred."[33] G.K.C. felt that the only realistic view of government must take into account the true, sinful nature of man, such as the founders of the American and French Revolutions did.

Chesterton was clear that the American and French Revolutions had been betrayed by party politics and self-serving oligarchies, but his primary interest was always England. What he wanted for England was nothing less than a revolution as well. In fact, his view of the public life of England in his day was of a struggle between opposing revolutions. He wrote,

> [T]here are two revolutions. And I saw that the whole mad modern world is a race between them. Which will happen first—the revolution in which bad things shall perish, or that other revolution in which good things shall perish also? One is the riot that all good men, even the most conservative, really dream of, when the sneer shall be struck from the face of the well-fed; when the wine of honour shall be poured down the throat of despair; when we shall, so far as to the sons of flesh is possible, take tyranny and usury and public treason and bind them into bundles and burn them.[34]

The third count which Chesterton raised against the English plutocracy was that it was thoroughly corrupt. "There is really a vast amount of corruption and hypocrisy in our election politics,"[35] wrote G.K.C. in a nonfiction setting; and a character in his novel *The Flying Inn* recites these lines with regard to Parliament:

> While flows the sacred river,
> While stands the sacred hill,
> The proud old pantaloons and nincompoops
> Who yawn at the very length of their own lies
> in that accursed sanhedrin where
> people put each other's hats on in a poisonous room
> with no more windows than hell,
> Shall have such honor still.[36]

Chesterton felt that the political party system attracted the worst sort of men. "I doubt," he wrote, "whether the best men ever would devote themselves to politics. The best men devote themselves to pigs and babies and things like that."[37] And the pomp and trappings of government only served as a cover for the wretchedness. "As you will not try to make the best people the most powerful people," he quipped with some sarcasm, "persuade yourselves that the most powerful people are the best people."[38]

An incident that perhaps plunged Gilbert Chesterton into the world of politics more immediately than any other was the Marconi scandal and the subsequent trial of Cecil Chesterton on charges of libel. Though throughout their lifetimes the brothers Chesterton had found complete agreement on few topics, the Marconi case brought them together in battle against flagrant political corruption and attempted cover-up in high public office.

The Chestertons and their friend Hilaire Belloc had long been outspoken critics of the party sytem in English politics. In his essays, Gilbert had often referred to the dishonesty inherent in political parties.

> [T]he English party system is founded upon the principle that telling the whole truth does not matter. It is founded upon the principle that half a truth is better than no politics. Our system deliberately turns a crowd of men who might be impartial into irrational partisans. It teaches some of them to tell lies and all of them to believe lies.[39]

Indeed, Cecil Chesterton and Hilaire Belloc became so engrossed by the problem that they collaborated on a book called *The Party System*, advancing the thesis that the English political parties were an irrelevant sideshow, and that the government was actually run by a small plutocracy of the most important men in both parties for their own personal interests. This book was received so enthusiastically in some quarters that a few supporters instituted a weekly paper called the *Eye-Witness*, with Belloc as editor and Cecil Chesterton as subeditor.

In the process of its untiring efforts to expose political corruption, the *Eye-Witness* managed to uncover a situation in which certain government ministers had received a tip to purchase shares in the Marconi company, whose contract with the government was at that time under consideration. When the weekly paper made its accusations public, the politicians first claimed that there was no substance to the rumors.

However, under continued investigation and pressure from the press, a story unfolded in which the government did, in fact, grant to the Marconi company a monopoly on setting up a nationwide communication system. What became particularly newsworthy were the facts that the managing director of the Marconi Company was

Mr. Godfrey Isaacs, the brother of the Attorney General, and that Mr. Lloyd George and other government Ministers had indeed bought shares in the American branch of the Marconi Company before the contract was awarded.

Meanwhile Cecil Chesterton had inherited the editorship of the weekly paper, which he now called the *New Witness*. And with renewed zeal Cecil mounted an unrelenting attack on the Isaacs brothers, which culminated in Mr. Godfrey Isaacs' taking him to court for personal libel. The trial and its publicity served to expose the dishonesty and the cover-up even more widely in the public eye, and meanwhile Gilbert Chesterton used every opportunity in his own writing to expose and condemn the corruption in government that seemed increasingly to be taken for granted.

The end of the affair for the Chestertons was bittersweet. Though the guilt of the politicians was established beyond a doubt, Cecil Chesterton was indeed found guilty of libel nevertheless and had to pay a small token fine to the courts. But the political outcome was particularly hard for the Chestertons to swallow, for it verified their worst predictions that corruption was becoming an accepted part of English politics and that the thesis of *The Party System* was only too true.

The essence of the political problem was to G.K.C. the same as of the individual person:

> We have lost the idea of repentance; especially in public things;
> that is why we cannot really get rid of our great national abuses
> of economic tyranny and aristocratic avarice.[40]

Repentance means to admit that we are wrong—that we are sinful creatures, that we tend toward greed and pride—and to embark upon a renewed course in the right direction. England needed to repent its corrupt oligarchy and to restore the true democracy implied by Christian doctrine. Chesterton wrote, "... the only logical negation of oligarchy was in the affirmation of original sin."[41] In other words, only under the false premise that an elite few are superior beings can oligarchies survive; only by the creed that all men are prone to corruption can true democracy stand.

The fourth count that Chesterton raised against the English plutocracy was that they were anti-English. Chesterton was ever the English patriot, and as such he wanted not only the best for England, but also for England to be the best it could be. He held these views not in the superficial sense of the jingo, but in a deeper, moral sense of what England stood for domestically and among the nations. Some questioned Chesterton's patriotism on the grounds that he was often so critical of the English government; G.K.C. defended his patriotism on the grounds that he was always for the common people of England.

From about 1870 into the first decade of the 20th century, the nations of western Europe—and particularly Great Britain—extended their power over the peoples of Africa and the Orient. Rapid advances in science and industry were utilized in Europe to develop advanced new war technologies, which were quickly transformed into political power. This power—combined with a desire for more raw materials, natural resources, and new markets for manufactured goods—spurred expansion into previously untouched areas of the world.

This extension of authority and control over entire geographic areas and peoples is called *imperialism*, and nowhere was it more enthusiastically pursued than in Great Britain. Indeed, the poet and storyteller Rudyard Kipling became a famous champion of imperialism, with his line: "Take up the White Man's burden . . . ." In just six years under Prime Minister Disraeli, England annexed Fiji and Cypress, fought the Zulus in Africa, purchased shares in the Suez Canal, and claimed England's Queen Victoria as "Empress of India." Eventually the British Empire would extend literally around the globe—including Egypt, Somaliland, Bechuanaland, East Africa, South Africa, Sudan, Gambia, Sierra Leone, Gold Coast, Nigeria, Persia, India, New Zealand, Australia, Canada, and others.

Popular thinking in England tended to equate English patriotism with enthusiasm for the British Empire. However, G. K. Chesterton took issue. According to G.K.C. and friends, there was nothing at all patriotic about building a British Empire, and he was emphatically against such a project. He wrote,

> To us it seemed obvious that Patriotism and Imperialism were not only not the same thing, but very nearly opposite things. But it did not seem obvious, but very puzzling, to the great majority of healthy patriots and innocent Imperialists.[42]

And he explained imperialism as he saw it:

It is the attempt of a European country to create a kind of sham Europe which it can dominate, instead of the real Europe, which it can only share. . . . I do not believe in Imperialism as commonly understood. I think it not merely an occasional wrong to other peoples but a continuous feebleness, a running sore, in my own.[43]

Chesterton's opposition to a British Empire was based on two foundations: his English patriotism and his Christian faith. This man who loved England did not like what he saw happening to England as it pursued the imperial course. He wrote, "I did not want England to be a sort of cloakroom or clearing-house for luggage labelled exports and imports."[44] Chesterton wanted England to be the more free, more agrarian nation it had been before the mania for industrial capitalism had seized its imagination.

But there was also the moral question. In an age in which modern sophisticates were so proudly rejecting traditional norms and values, Chesterton was unabashed in his insistence on Christian morality even in foreign policy. When he referred to imperialism as "a continuous feebleness, a running sore"[45] in England, he was saying that to subjugate and exploit other peoples is not only to dehumanize them, but to degrade oneself.

To G. K. Chesterton the issue again was human dignity. Men and women were created in the image of God, and to dominate, abuse, and exploit them was an offense against their Creator. The apologists of imperialism tried to remove human beings from the picture by appealing to inevitable natural processes and sweeping historical forces. The capitalists appealed to natural selection and inexorable progress; the socialists appealed to historical dialectics and the collective state. Both sought the subordination of the individual person to the powers of inevitable change.

In this regard, Chesterton wrote,

The two great movements during my youth and early manhood were Imperialism and Socialism. They were supposed to be fighting each other; and so doubtless they did, in the sense of waving Red Flags against Union Jacks. But as compared with those dim gropings in my own imagination, the two things were in union. . . . Both believed in unification and centralization on a large scale.[46]

Those "dim gropings" were Chesterton's early discoveries of what he later came to realize was simply Christian doctrine: that each and every individual human being is a special creation of God and is therefore worthy of being treated with justice and dignity.

So in Chesterton's view, imperialism was nothing more than the political and geographic expansion of those same unjust and dehumanizing forces that were the heartbeat of the industrial expansion at home. Whether capitalist or socialist, the effect was the same—the lives of real men and women were defined and controlled by impersonal ideas and plans which denied them the opportunity to make the free choices for which they were created. In short, imperialism was bad for England, and bad for people everywhere.

But what about Ireland? One may well ask the British anti-imperialist if his ideals can also encompass the English domination of its Irish neighbor. And here G.K.C. was indeed consistent. Again taking the highly unpopular stand, he came out unequivocally in favor of home rule for Ireland. "I have always felt it the first duty of a real English patriot to sympathize with the passionate patriotism of Ireland," he wrote.[47] For again it was the Christian idea of human dignity that guided even his concept of patriotism. Chesterton felt that Christian doctrine supported a strong and healthy loyalty to one's own homeland, and what was fair for the English should certainly have been fair for the Irish.

But nowhere was Chesterton's patriotism more bitterly questioned than with regard to his views on the Boer War in 1899–1900. G.K.C. possessed a very strong sense of patriotism for his native England, and he expected good men and women everywhere to possess equally strong loyalties to their own homelands. Therefore it was only consistent that he felt a measure of sympathy with the patriotism of the Boers, even though his own English government was waging an imperialistic war against them in South Africa.

But to understand the Boer War we must begin in 1806 when Great Britain first acquired the colony of South Africa from the Dutch. The Dutch people in South Africa, called Boers, were a proud and independent sort, and there were conflicts with the British from the start.

In 1834 the Boers began the "Great Trek," a migration in ox-drawn carts into the interior to establish two independent homelands far from British interference. These states they named "Transvaal" and "Orange Free State." But British control eventually extended northward as well, surrounding the Boer states on all sides. There was much fighting and bloodshed between the Boers and the native Africans, and the British finally intervened. In the early 1850s the British signed two treaties with the Boers. But from 1860 to 1885 tensions increased again, and when Britain tried to annex Transvaal, hostilities broke out. Transvaal and the Boers managed to surprise and defeat a small British army, and so England again recognized Transvaal as an independent state.

Then gold was discovered in Transvaal. Foreigners, or Uitlanders, flooded the area, and soon Johannesburg swelled to a population of 100,000, many of whom were British. Paul Kruger, the President of Transvaal, distrusted the British, and heavy taxes were levied on all Uitlanders. Meanwhile, British capitalist Cecil Rhodes, who was in the process of becoming extremely wealthy on South African gold and diamonds, plotted with other Uitlanders to overthrow the government of Transvaal. The plot failed and was exposed, and war between the Boers and the British broke out in 1899.

Back in London most of the government officials and journalists were promoting the South African War as a noble British cause. The popular sentiment was simply that England had an enemy, so patriotism would have good Britons cheering for Britain. But here was where Chesterton and a few others took issue. Yes, England was making war against an enemy, but the problem as Chesterton saw it was that in this case England happened to be wrong. And as a matter of true patriotism, he could not wave the flag and cheer when his country was in the wrong.

Consequently, Chesterton took the highly unpopular public stance of being pro-Boer. The Boers, he felt, had every natural right to fight to protect their country from outsiders. They had every right to resist the greedy tentacles of empire-builders like Cecil Rhodes. And they had every right to try to prevent Uitlanders from carrying away their natural resources. Chesterton wrote, "the Boers might be making a noise (with Mauser rifles) but I thought it was a noise on the right side."[48]

Chesterton felt that the real impetus behind British involvement in the South African War was simply greed. The motives of Cecil Rhodes were certainly clear enough, and the widespread adoration of empire-building among the British worked to make the English public solidly in favor of subduing the Boers militarily. Even the

Fabian Socialists seemed to favor the campaign. Chesterton explained,

> As compared with Belloc or myself, Bernard Shaw was definitely
> in favor of the South African War.... [H]e defends the only sort
> of war I thoroughly despise, the bullying of small states for their
> oil or gold; and he despises the only sort of war that I really defend,
> a war of civilizations and religions, to determine the moral destiny
> of mankind.[49]

Chesterton was never a pacifist, but he was clear and strong in his belief that wars should be fought over higher principles than protecting the monetary interests of millionaires.

But the taproot of Chesterton's opposition to the British cause against the Boers went even deeper than his moral conception of patriotism; it reached on down into the bedrock of Christian doctrine. For G.K.C. had always argued that Christianity was the only creed that really questioned the right of the strong to dominate the weak. And against the flood of jingoism and the justifying slogans of "survival of the fittest" and "manifest destiny" regarding the Boer War, Chesterton asserted, "Only the Christian Church can offer any rational objection to a complete confidence in the rich."[50]

When the war first broke out in 1899 the world was surprised to see the Boers hand the British army several shocking defeats. But in time England sent the necessary manpower and equipment to defeat the Boers by the end of the next year. So despite the protests of Chesterton, the British cause was pushed and won in South Africa, opening the entire area for exploitation by Cecil Rhodes and others. In 1909 the former Dutch and English states were united to form the Union of South Africa.

In his *Autobiography* Chesterton summarized a major guiding principle behind his political thoughts as follows:

> It was my instinct to defend liberty in small nations and poor
> families; that is, to defend the rights of man as including the rights
> of property; especially the property of the poor. I did not really
> understand what I meant by liberty, until I heard it called by the
> name of Human Dignity.[51]

The Christian concept of human dignity is based on the doctrine that all people of all nations were created in the very image of God. Chesterton's approach to the politics, economics, and sociology of modern human relations never allowed that human dignity to be shunted to the sidelines—and this fact explains his vigorous opposition to nearly every "ism" of the 19th and 20th centuries. Chesterton felt that Christian doctrine was the only philosophy that included a moral basis for individual human dignity.

Men and women were not created for the purpose of being pawns in the power games of an elite few, nor of being cogs in some great machine of progress, nor of being cells in some collective organism of the future. They were created in the very image of their Creator—capable of rational thought and moral choice, and thus, of liberty. G.K.C. wrote,

> Generally, the moral substance of liberty is this: that man is not meant merely to receive good laws, good food, or good conditions, like a tree in a garden, but is meant to take a certain princely pleasure in selecting and shaping, like the gardener.[52]

Here, then, was the foundation of G. K. Chesterton's social and political thoughts—the key to the Christian revolution. "To the orthodox there must always be a case for revolution," Chesterton wrote in *Orthodoxy*, "for in the hearts of men God has been put under the feet of Satan. In the upper world hell once rebelled against heaven. But in this world heaven is rebelling against hell."[53]

8

Consorting in Fairyland

G. K. Chesterton sometimes stated that he believed in elves and fairies. Often this statement was taken as a merely rhetorical device for confounding the arguments of his opponents and providing a basis for his arguments on religion. Sometimes the statement was taken somewhat metaphorically to represent Chesterton's rejection of the strictly materialist worldview. But as one digs deeper into Chesterton's comments on elves and fairies, one comes to realize a more profound sense in which the statement was literally true.

It is true that most of his references to fairyland occurred in the context of Chesterton's arguments against materialist philosophy. But his thoughts on the world of elves and fairies were by no means rhetorical devices or mere sophistry. They were instead a reflection of his deeply held view that the visible, physical world presents the rather dull backside of the richer, more vivid reality that is hidden from our sight.

Those who are tempted to dismiss Chesterton's preference for fairyland as a frivolous metaphor soon find that he was in this regard as serious as ever. In his book *Orthodoxy* he explained,

> The things I believed most then, the things I believe most now, are the things called fairy tales. They seem to me to be the entirely reasonable things. They are not fantasies: compared with them other things are fantastic.[1]

Again as in the case of Chesterton's humor, his thoughts on fairyland were firmly grounded in his rejection of the deadening and blinding effects of mechanistic materialism and in his affirmation of the vivifying and joyous effects of the reality behind the physical facade.

In his *Autobiography* Chesterton traced his own appreciation of fairyland back to the writings of Robert Louis Stevenson, William Butler Yeats, and especially to "the glamorous mysticism of George Macdonald."[2] It was from the stories of George MacDonald that G.K.C. learned to look for the spiritual meaning behind the objects and events in the visible world. He learned to see that material things possess within them a kind of magic; or, as Chesterton scholar Ian Boyd explained it, the "exterior material reality is a disguise for its inner spiritual splendour."[3]

Chesterton's appreciation for the poetry of William Butler Yeats was in part due to Yeats' turning of the tables on the materialists. G.K.C. wrote,

> Yeats stood for enchantment.... He was the real original rationalist who said that the fairies stand to reason. He staggered the materialists by attacking their abstract materialism with a completely concrete mysticism.[4]

We have seen how Chesterton used this approach in his arguments against the "mythologies" of the scientific evolutionists and in favor of the rational nature of Christian doctrine. In Chesterton's own words, "I was all for fighting for Willie Yeats and his fairies against materialism."[5]

And Chesterton's admiration for Robert Louis Stevenson was boundless. In Stevenson G.K.C. saw an intrinsic joy that came from an understanding of the greater, spiritual nature of things. Chesterton wrote,

> Stevenson's enormous capacity for joy flowed directly out of his profoundly religious temperament.... It was the greater gaiety of the mystic. He could enjoy trifles, because to him there was no such thing as a trifle. He was a child who respected his dolls because they were the images of the image of God.[6]

Chesterton held that Robert Louis Stevenson was the embodiment of an "elvish sanity,"[7] which perceived the greater reality in the world beyond the material facade.

We begin to see the meaning of Chesterton's own thoughts on fairyland in his little play called *Magic*. Here G.K.C. clearly set his stage with representative types, including the Doctor, representing the overconfidence of empirical science; the Duke, representing the muddleheaded progressivism of the upper classes; the Reverend Smith, representing the sophistic agnosticism of the modern clergy; Patricia Carleon, representing a native Irish mysticism; her American brother Morris Carleon, representing a cocksure and militant type of materialism, who comes into inevitable combat with the mysterious Conjurer, who carries the author's true meaning into the play.

Briefly, the play *Magic* presents a situation where the Duke has invited the Conjurer to do magic tricks to entertain his visiting niece and nephew, the Carleons. The Conjurer arrives unannounced in the garden, wherein the dreamy Patricia takes him for an actual fairy and is of course very disappointed to find later that he is simply a magician hired by her uncle. The protective and materialist brother Morris, on the other hand, challenges the honor of the Conjurer with such aggression that the Conjurer actually appeals to the powers of dark magic to confound the young man.

When the contemptuous Morris finds that he cannot explain away the Conjurer's final trick, he begins to lose his wits, to go mad, and is immediately put to bed by the Doctor, who leaves him under the watchful care of his sister. Here is where Chesterton's purposes begin to reveal themselves, as the various representative characters discuss what has transpired.

At first it is Smith, the clergyman, who argues the case against the materialist empiricism of the Doctor and Morris:

> Smith: . . . Why should sham miracles prove to us that real Saints and Prophets never lived. There may be sham magic and real magic also. . . . There may be turnip ghosts precisely because there are real ghosts. There may be theatrical fairies precisely because there are real fairies. You do not abolish the Bank of England by pointing to a forged bank note.[8]

Chesterton used the events and arguments of the play to establish a case for the existence of the supernatural and for the fact that a strict materialist philosophy leads in the end to madness.

Subsequent conversations among the characters then provide insights on the scientist, the progressive, and the agnostic clergyman each in his turn. It is the clergyman Smith who confronts the Doctor. Upon learning that the Doctor has left the ailing Morris under the care of Patricia, the dreamy spiritualist, Smith retorts,

> Smith: His sister! Oh, then you do believe in fairies?
>
> Doctor: Believe in fairies? What do you mean?
>
> Smith: At least you put the person who does believe in them in charge of the person who doesn't.
>
> Doctor: Well, I suppose I do.

Smith: You don't think she'll keep him awake all night with fairy tales?

Doctor: Certainly not.

Smith: You don't think she'll throw the medicine bottle out the window and administer—er—a dewdrop or anything of that sort? Or a four-leaved clover, say?

Doctor: No, of course not.

Smith: I only ask because you scientific men are a little hard on us clergymen. You don't believe in a priesthood; but you'll admit I'm more really a priest than this conjurer is really a magician. . . . But Miss Carleon believed in the wizard. Miss Carleon believed in the language of the elves. And you put her in charge of an invalid without a flicker of doubt.[9]

Chesterton's point, which is understandably not developed very completely in this short play, is that the theories and notions of science often contain elements that are far from the strictly rational and empirical, often seeming very close to a belief in a kind of "magic."

And so the dialogue goes through the vague and popular creeds of the long-winded Duke, who delivers an incessant string of phrases like, "Progress, you know, progress!" and, "That's where I take the larger views!" And having referred to all of the popular ideas on progress and evolution and larger laws of things, the Duke draws the line at believing in magic:

Duke: Why, really, magic. . .

Conjurer: Yes, your Grace, one of those larger laws you were telling us about.[10]

In his arguments with the scientific and economic determinists Chesterton was forever pointing out the "magic" implied in concepts like "natural selection" and the "invisible hand" of competition, and the muddleheaded Duke is Chesterton's vehicle for showing the irony in such a person disbelieving in magic.

And finally there is the clergyman, the Reverend Smith, who so cleverly argues against the scientific empiricists, but whose rather pragmatic agnosticism begins to emerge from his rhetoric:

Doctor: Do you believe in your own religion?

Smith: Suppose I don't. I should still be a fool to question it. The child who doubts Santa Claus has insomnia. The child who believes has a good night's rest.

Doctor: You are a Pragmatist.[11]

But it is the Conjurer, the one universally denounced as a mere trickster, who goes to the heart of the clergyman's hypocrisy.

Conjurer: I will take my cloak off when you take off your coat.

Smith: Why? Do you want me to fight?

Conjurer: I want you to be martyred. I want you to bear witness to your own creed. I say these things are supernatural. I say this was done by a spirit. The doctor does not believe me. He is an agnostic; and he knows everything. The Duke does not believe me; he cannot believe anything so plain as a miracle. But what the devil are you for, if you don't believe in a miracle? What does your coat mean, if it doesn't mean that there is such a thing as the supernatural? What does your cursed collar mean if it doesn't mean there is such a thing as a spirit? Why the devil do you dress up like that if you don't believe in it?[12]

And so having dismissed the popular agnostic creeds of the day, Chesterton's play comes to its moment of truth when the others convince the Conjurer that he must tell them exactly how he accomplished his last trick. The Duke even writes him a large check in exchange for telling the secret. But the Conjurer is reticent to tell, warning them several times that at any rate they will not believe him. Finally he tells them that he regrettably accomplished the final trick by resorting to real magic. They do not believe him.

Doctor: Do you really mean that you take the cheque and then tell us it was only magic?

Conjurer: (Pulling the cheque to pieces) I tear the cheque, and I tell you it was only magic.

Doctor: But hang it all, there's no such thing.

Conjurer: Yes there is. I wish to God I did not know that there is.[13]

Yes, there is magic, says Chesterton through his Conjurer, but what is the nature of this magic? Why does he "wish to God" he did not know about it? In explaining himself to Patricia Carleon, with whom he has now fallen in love, the Conjuror says, "How I did that trick? I did it by devils. You could believe in fairies. Can't you believe in devils?"[14] And he tells how his seemingly innocent dabbling in spiritualism led him into trouble.

> They turned the tables. They turned the tables on me. I don't wonder at your believing in fairies. As long as these things were my servants they seemed to me like fairies. When they tried to be my masters .... I found they were not fairies. I found the spirits with whom I at least had come in contact were evil ... awfully, unnaturally evil.[15]

And so G.K.C. asserted the reality not only of the supernatural, but of supernatural good and evil; and among his characters it is only the repentant Conjurer who knows their reality.

Finally, disgusted at himself for having resorted to evil power and having sent the young Morris toward madness, the Conjurer exits to the garden.

> Doctor: Where are you going?
>
> Conjurer: I am going to ask the God whose enemies I have served if I am still worthy to save a child.[16]

Here is the turning point in Christian doctrine. Here is the unworthy and repentant sinner appealing to the merciful God to remove his guilt and make him worthy to serve the good.

In the play we are not privy to the Conjurer's conversation with God in the garden, but we are shown the results of the man's repentance. In his pride the Conjurer had been goaded by the obnoxious Morris into doing something truly supernatural; in his humility he is required to do one of the most difficult things conceivable—to go and tell Morris he was right, that there is a rational-empirical explanation to the last trick. Morris needs this lie to keep from going mad; the Conjurer needs it as an antidote for his pride.

But in the end fairyland is intact and Patricia's dreamy mysticism is vindicated. There is much more to reality than materialist philosophy will admit or empirical methods can perceive, and Patricia and the Conjurer are the only ones who understand this truth. Each of them had harbored their own fairy tales about loving the other, and in the end they do find that they are in love.

> Patricia: That fairy tale has really and truly come to an end. It is

very hard for a fairy tale to come to an end. If you leave it alone it lingers everlastingly. Our fairy tale has come to an end in the only way a fairy tale can come to an end. The only way a fairy tale can leave off being a fairy tale.

Conjurer: I don't understand you.

Patricia: It has come true.[17]

In this way G. K. Chesterton's little play ends on a note of connection between fairyland and the conscious life which we call reality. His protagonists have asserted the reality of the supernatural—of spirits and of devils—and the unreality and hypocrisy of the materialists, the empiricists, the progressives, and the determinists. Here the play develops one of Chesterton's recurrent themes: the narrowness of the materialist atheist creed. "There is no bigot like the atheist," his Conjurer says,[18] and the play *Magic* is an exposition of that atheistic bigotry.

Chesterton's mysticism was by necessity a militant mysticism, which directed much of its fury against those forces that sought to destroy it. Here, in fact, was the very spirit of his dogged opposition to the pervasive pseudo-scientific ethos. For many sought to dismiss with the wave of a hand and a sneer the magical, the wonderful, the surprising in nature; and then to claim to have "explained away" that which is truly marvelous and unexplicable. Chesterton wrote,

> But the scientific men do muddle their heads, until they imagine a necessary connection between an apple leaving the tree and an apple reaching the ground. They really do talk as if they had found not only a set of marvellous facts, but a truth connecting those facts. . . . They feel that because one incomprehensible thing constantly follows another incomprehensible thing the two together somehow make up a comprehensible thing. . . . But we cannot say why an egg can turn into a chicken any more than we can say why a bear could turn into a fairy prince. . . . When we are asked why eggs turn into birds or fruits fall in autumn, we must answer exactly as the fairy godmother would answer if Cinderella asked her why mice turned into horses or her clothes fell from her at twelve o'clock. We must answer that it is magic.[19]

Though learned people so blithely speak of "the law of gravity" and "genetic coding" and other scientific facts, few stop to remember that much of our science is mere description, classification, and labeling. Nobody really seems to know, for instance, *why* gravity works as it does, and Chesterton was not unreasonable in calling it "magic."

We saw earlier that one of Chesterton's chief complaints against the scientific worldview was that it deadened the mind to what is beautiful, what is romantic, what is pleasurable in the ordinary things around us. In his play *Magic* G.K.C. put the deadening, materialist words in the voice of the Doctor, speaking to the dreamy Patricia.

> Doctor: . . . dream for us who can dream no longer. But do not quite forget the difference.
>
> Patricia: What difference?
>
> Doctor: The difference between the things that are beautiful and the things that are true. That red lamp over my door isn't beautiful; but it's there.[20]

In relegating the poetry and romance of life to another distinctly separate realm—an inferior and somehow less real realm—the scientific materialists create a world where even beauty and joy become a tolerable irrelevancy at best.

And yet Chesterton argued that the romance, the beauty, the incredible surprises are there all around us; but that we have so damaged and blunted our own perception as to be unable to see them anymore. Writing about G.K. Chesterton, Ian Boyd explained,

> For him, the material world in which human beings live is still the Garden of Eden: but because of the Fall, human eye-sight has been so damaged that it is no longer capable of recognizing paradise.[21]

Even the "cold facts" that we have been taught to label and take for granted contain marvelous wonders. G.K.C. held that if it weren't for our acquired blindness, the mere facts around us would make our knees knock with religious fear—we would understand that every instant of our conscious life is an unimaginable prodigy.

In poking fun at the too literal, too antipoetic element in the scientific society, Chesterton included a rhyme in his collection *Greybeards at Play,* which was titled "The Literal Land." It reads in part:

> If you should call your children "pigs"
> because they bite their nails

> The incautious word will fill the room
> with squeaks and curly tails.
> A man once said "the lion's share"
> with metaphoric pride;
> He was eaten by his metaphor—
> which is undignified.[22]

Again, the real point is that trying to rid the world of metaphor, of poetry, of romance, of spirit leads in the end to a kind of madness. G.K.C. explained, "Facts as facts do not always create a spirit of reality, because reality is a spirit. Facts by themselves can often feed the flame of madness, because sanity is a spirit."[23]

And so, Chesterton's belief in fairyland was in part a belief in joy—in romance, in surprise, in adventure, in poetry, in wonder. The trick, according to G.K.C., was to regain the ability to see and to be amazed. In this regard he wrote,

> Now, if there is one thing of which I have been certain since my boyhood, and grew more certain as I advance in age, it is that nothing is poetical if plain daylight is not poetical; and no monster should amaze us if the normal man does not amaze.[24]

And again,

> The supreme adventure is being born. There we do walk suddenly into a splendid and startling trap. There we do see something of which we have not dreamed before. Our father and mother do lie in wait for us and leap out on us, like brigands from a bush. Our uncle is a surprise. Our aunt is, in the beautiful common expression, a bolt from the blue. When we step into the family, by the act of being born, we do step into a world which is incalculable, into a world which has its own strange laws, into a world which could do without us, into a world that we have not made. In other words, when we step into the family we step into a fairytale.[25]

There are strange and amazing things everywhere around us, said Chesterton, and our joy depends upon our ability to perceive and appreciate these things.

"How can we contrive," G.K.C. once asked, "to be astonished at the world and yet at home in it?"[26] Chesterton was aware that human wonder and joy are problematic: in our present fallen state we are ill-equipped to appreciate the wonders around us. We have trained ourselves through our philosophies to perceive only the faded backside of life; we have trained ourselves through our sciences merely to shrug, label, and classify even the most marvelous of phenomena. And yet, he wrote,

> The aim of life is appreciation; there is no sense in not appreciating things; and there is no sense in having more of them if you have less appreciation of them.[27]

Here again is the appeal to sense; it is simply irrational not to let oneself be astonished. To Chesterton the "rational" and the "wonderful" are not exclusive categories—they belong to one another.

And Chesterton claimed that men and women were created with a divine capacity of enjoyment:

> At the back of our brains, so to speak, there was a forgotten blaze or burst of astonishment at our own existence. The object of the artistic and spiritual life was to dig for this submerged sunrise of wonder; so that a man sitting in a chair might suddenly understand that he was actually alive, and be happy.[28]

Though the capacity is there, the philosophies and creeds of modernism are stacked unanimously against our realizing our own enjoyment.

> In short, it seems to me, it matters very little whether a man is discontented in the name of pessimism or progress, if his discontent does in fact paralyse his power of appreciating what he has got. The real difficulty of man is not to enjoy lamp-posts or landscapes, not to enjoy dandelions or chops; but to enjoy enjoyment. To keep the capacity of really liking what he likes; that is the practical problem which the philosopher has to solve.[29]

In Chesterton's view, all of the modern philosophies had failed to solve the riddle of human joy.

If human joy was indeed a riddle, it was a riddle with a solution—there was a way to its solution. And G.K.C. again appealed to the reasonableness of fairyland for clues. Essential among the "strange laws" of fairyland was that joy is always found within limits or conditions. Chesterton explained,

> For the pleasure of pedantry I will call it the Doctrine of Conditional Joy ... according to elfin ethics all virtue is in an "if." The note of the fairy utterance always is, "You may live in a palace of

gold and sapphire, *if* you do not say the word 'cow' . . ." The vision always hangs upon a veto. All the dizzy and colossal things conceded depend upon one small thing withheld. . . . In the fairy tale an incomprehensible happiness rests upon an incomprehensible condition.[30]

Or perhaps in more prosaic language,

The thing which keeps life romantic and full of fiery possibilities is the existence of these great plain limitations which force all of us to meet the things we do not like or do not expect. It is vain for the supercilious moderns to talk of being in uncongenial surroundings. To be in a romance is to be in uncongenial surroundings. To be born into this earth is to be born into uncongenial surroundings, hence to be born into a romance.[31]

Chesterton developed more fully this theme that peace and happiness can only exist on some condition in the essay on fairy tales in his book *All Things Considered.*

It is clear that G.K.C.'s thoughts on conditional joy are grounded in the Christian doctrine of humanity's temptation and fall in the Garden of Eden. The story of Eden is the prototype for all stories of human happiness and unhappiness, and to Chesterton there was no mystery in the fact that a similar theme emerges repeatedly in the fairy tales of all times and places. The warning not to eat of the certain fruit is the eternal prohibition; the lies and excuses in the temptation are a million "good" reasons to ignore the divine prohibition.

The hedonisms of the modern world claim that human joy is to be found in throwing off all traditional prohibitions—often inaccurately called "repression" and "guilt"—and instead "freeing" oneself to do whatever one desires to do. But Chesterton argued that human beings are not really made that way; their true pleasure is to be found in honoring the divine prohibition.

Strike a glass, and it will not endure an instant; simply do not strike it, and it will endure a thousand years. Such, it seemed, was the joy of man, either in elfland or on earth; the happiness depended on *not doing something* which you could at any moment do and which, very often, it was not obvious why you should not do.[32]

With the advantage of hindsight, we are often able to see why we should not have struck the glass, but such foresight is a different matter. In our arrogance we distrust the wisdom of the ages and insist on breaking our lives for the hollow privilege of saying, "I did it my way."

So in this context we have again returned to the dominant theme in Chesterton's thoughts on hearing God's laughter. And the theme is that it is in humility and gratefulness that joy is found—that there is a divine wisdom in quieting our pride and listening carefully to the ancient limits and prohibitions. It is the "law of elfland" which says that if we heed the warning of the fairy godmother and choose *not* to do what is prohibited, then we shall indeed enjoy the wonders promised.

Now, all of this discussion of fairyland and the laws of elfland may tempt the reader to conclude that G.K.C. was, after all, merely dealing in figures of speech and metaphorical language, but the fact is that Chesterton could not have been more serious in his intentions. For it was a matter of ontological importance to him that there was a reality that was not only metaphysical, but was even more valid, more vivid, and more vital than the material reality understood by ordinary human perceptions.

It was this *sacramental mysticism* which G.K.C. had learned largely from the stories of George MacDonald, and which the Protestant writer C. S. Lewis shared as well. It is a point of view that is explained more fully by Ian Boyd, editor of *The Chesterton Review,* in his article, "Chesterton and C. S. Lewis."[33] The essence of this sacramental perspective is the belief that our physical and conscious existence is itself a sacrament —that is, a visible representation of things sacred. As such, the events of our daily lives are in a more profound reality the acting out of the moral struggle between good and evil.

It is important to realize that Chesterton's sacramental view was not an other-worldly spiritualism that relegated the profane realm to unimportance. In fact, in this sacramental view the physical world takes on an even greater significance as the very embodiment of the deeper spiritual entities. Consequently, G.K.C. saw in ordinary things and people the mystical and moral struggles of the spiritual universe. In this sense, material things deceive the perceptions by being far more real than they appear to be.

This sacramental vision was illustrated in the character Evan

MacIan in Chesterton's novel *The Ball and the Cross*. The author wrote of MacIan that "all through his life he thought of the daylight world as a sort of divine debris, the broken remainder of his first vision."[34] And this same "divine debris" is found in the thoughts of the poet Dorian Wimpole in the novel *The Flying Inn*:

> Cloudily there crowded into his mind ideas with which he was imperfectly familiar, especially an idea which he had heard called "The Image of God." It seemed to him more and more that all these things, from the donkey to the very docks and ferns by the roadside, were dignified and sanctified by their partial resemblance to something else.[35]

Thus, the sacramental view might be stated as understanding that our senses are perceiving the "divine debris," the physical substances of the spiritual reality behind them.

"The Image of God," of course, refers to humans. And this sacramental attitude toward his fellow human beings was the basis of Chesterton's arguments in sociology and politics, in that the abuse of any man or woman was in fact the abuse of a potentially divine creature. The forces that enslaved the poor and misled the populace were not simply economic or historical forces—they were the forces of a deeper, spiritual warfare upon the souls of men and women. They were, in fact, the forces of evil.

There is in the concept of the "divine debris" a sense of something lost and of something good to be preserved. In *Orthodoxy* G.K.C. wrote,

> My sense that happiness hung on the crazy thread of a condition did mean something when all was said: it meant the whole doctrine of the Fall. . . . And my haunting instinct that somehow good was not merely a tool to be used, but a relic to be guarded, like the goods from Crusoe's ship—even that had been the wild whisper of something originally wise, for, according to Christianity, we were indeed the survivors of a wreck, the crew of the golden ship that had gone down before the beginning of the world.[36]

The sacramental view looks behind the ordinary for the "divine debris," for the good which is "a remnant to be stored and held sacred out of some primordial ruin."[37] It gazes in wonder at the sacramental secret of the universe, and it responds in gratitude.

Chesterton concluded that "the proper form of thanks to it is some form of humility and restraint."[38]

And so, we begin to see more in Chesterton's passing comments on "a sacramental instinct within me ..."[39] or that the "... grass and garden trees seemed glittering with something at once good and unnatural, like a fire from fairyland ... ,"[40] now that we realize the sacramentalism in his view. Chesterton was most definitely not engaging in mere metaphor; his ventures into fairyland were an exploration of the profound reality hidden behind the material world.

Finally, as the events of his play *Magic* suggested, Chesterton felt that the very sanity of modern men and women hung upon the condition of their finding their way back to fairyland—their rediscovering the wonder of being alive. In his *Autobiography* he wrote,

> It was the problem of how men could be made to realize the wonder and splendour of being alive, in environments which their own daily criticism treated as dead-alive, and which their imagination had left for dead.[41]

In another context he wrote, "Mysticism keeps men sane."[42] For Chesterton the solution lay in the sacramental view of life, which—he was happy to point out—was the view of life that has been taught for nearly two millennia in the traditional doctrines of the Christian church.

9

Getting to the Heart
of Matters

In all of his writing, fiction and nonfiction, G. K. Chesterton had a great deal to say about politics, sociology, and philosophy. But all of his themes and theses in fiction and nonfiction contained a common thread running through them, and that common thread was engendered and informed by what Chesterton called orthodox Christian theology. In his masterpiece, *Orthodoxy,* Chesterton defined orthodox theology as basically that which is stated in the Apostles' Creed. Chesterton wrote,

> These essays are concerned only to discuss the actual fact that the central Christian theology (sufficiently summarized in the Apostles' Creed) is the best root of energy and sound ethics. They are not intended to discuss the very fascinating but quite different question of what is the present seat of authority for the proclamation of that creed. When the word "orthodoxy" is used here it means the Apostles' Creed, as understood by everybody calling himself Christian until a very short time ago and the general historic conduct of those who held such a creed.[1]

Thus casting controversies and denominations aside, Chesterton reduced his working definition of Christian theology to its logical and historical essence in the Apostles' Creed. And indeed, there is not a major Christian denomination of the Catholic or the Protestant persuasion that does not accept this ancient creed.

Given that G.K.C. based his entire intellectual output upon this creed and its implications, we include the statement of the creed in this final chapter on getting to the heart of matters. The standard Apostles' Creed reads like this:

I believe in God the Father Almighty, Maker of heaven and earth,

And in Jesus Christ his only Son our Lord; who was conceived by

the Holy Ghost, born of the Virgin Mary, suffered under Pontius
Pilate, was crucified, dead, and buried; he descended into hell;
the third day he rose again from the dead; he ascended into
heaven, and sitteth on the right hand of God the Father Almighty;
from thence he shall come to judge the quick and the dead.

I believe in the Holy Ghost; the holy catholic Church; the com-
munion of saints; the forgiveness of sins; the resurrection of the
body; and the life everlasting. Amen.

This creed is, so to speak, the Christian benchmark. These simple
statements represent the distillation of Christian doctrine, which has
resisted centuries of argument and attempts at revision. In Chesterton's view the Apostles' Creed is therefore an essential part of
the greatest wisdom passed along to the living from the grand democracy of those who have lived before us.

From the moment of its inception, the church of Jesus Christ
has been steeped in controversy. Scholars—both supporters and
detractors—through the ages have combed through the written rec-
ords and the church traditions, trying to unravel the enigmas, trying
to solve the riddles, trying to explain the paradoxes, trying to answer
the questions that abound about this man, Jesus of Nazareth, and
the church which he founded.

Each generation encounters Jesus in a new way, and each seems
to struggle in its own way with the various interpretations and implications of the creed. But in many cases the new ideas amount to
a rehashing of the old ideas that had already been tried and found
to be heretical to the true teachings of the church. This rehashing
of old heresies was, in fact, a major topic in Chesterton's book
Heretics and many of his other writings. But as G.K.C. was so fond
of pointing out, there can be no progress or improvement—in a
spiritual or intellectual or any other sense—if one refuses to consider the wisdom of the past and to build upon that solid foundation.

The church, wrote Chesterton, endures forever. Generations
come and go, controversies come and go, heresies are argued and
forgotten, and we might add that denominations split away and split
again. But the reality of the church of Jesus Christ remains. In his
novel *The Ball and the Cross,* Chesterton put these words into the
mouth of his protagonist, Evan MacIan:

"The Church is not a thing like the Athenaeum Club," he cried.

"If the Athenaeum Club lost all its members, the Athenaeum Club would dissolve and cease to exist. But when we belong to the Church we belong to something which is outside all of us; which is outside everything you talk about, outside the Cardinals and the Pope. They belong to it, but it does not belong to them. If we all fell dead suddenly, the Church would still somehow exist in God."[2]

It is this doctrine of the church as an established, spiritual entity that explains its perseverance through a history of opposition, division, scandal and persecution.

One of G. K. Chesterton's major theses was that the teachings of the Christian church are by no means merely dead superstitions of the past. "Theology," he once wrote, "is not (as some suppose) expunged as an error. It is merely concealed like a sin."[3] In another context he asserted this same idea, arguing this time from history itself:

If the medieval religion had really been such a silly superstition as some of its simpler enemies represent, it quite certainly *would* have been swallowed up forever in such an earthquake of enlightenment as the great Renaissance. The fact that the vision of a superb and many-sided human culture did not disturb the fundamental ideas of these late medieval Christians has a simple explanation: that the ideas are true.... It was the intellectual value of the creed that preserved it through any revolution of aesthetic values, just as it preserves it still amid the wildest changes in aesthetic taste to-day.[4]

In other words, if Christianity were really the silly myth that its detractors claim it to be, it would have ceased to exist long ago.

Chesterton was a defender of the faith in a literal sense. We have seen that his method of defense was often to take the offensive and cast the criticism back into the lap of the critic. He used this approach particularly in response to statements about the wrongs of the church. In one case he responded,

When people impute special vices to the Christian Church, they seem entirely to forget that the world ... has these vices much more. The Church has been cruel; but the world has been much more cruel. The Church has plotted; but the world has plotted much more. The Church has been superstitious; but it has never been so superstitious as the world is when left to itself.[5]

The point here was not to excuse the crimes of the church, but to hold its critics to a consistent standard of comparison.

In his "Authority and the Adventurer," the final chapter of his book, *Orthodoxy*, G.K.C. enumerated the most popular objections and arguments against the Christian church. He stated,

> If I am asked, as a purely intellectual question, why I believe in Christianity, I can only answer, "For the same reason that an intelligent agnostic disbelieves in Christianity." I believe in it quite rationally upon the evidence ... when I look at these various anti-Christian truths, I simply discover that none of them are true.[6]

He then went on to discuss the major criticisms and to bring his evidence to bear on the arguments. This is a chapter well worth reading, as is the entire book, *Orthodoxy*.

And finally with regard to the church in history, Chesterton often pointed to the roles that religion had fulfilled traditionally; such as helping people to understand the cosmos, teaching logic to students and fairy tales to children, confronting the gods of fear, and providing "a day for wearing ribbons or an hour for ringing bells."[7] Then looking at modern, urban-industrial life, Chesterton complained,

> The large uses of religion have been broken up into lesser specialties, just as the uses of the hearth have been broken up into hot water pipes and electric bulbs. The romance of ritual and coloured emblem has been taken over by that narrowest of all trades, modern art (the sort called art for art's sake), and men are in modern practice informed that they may use all symbols, so long as they mean nothing by them.
>
> The romance of conscience has been dried up into the science of ethics; which may well be called decency for decency's sake, decency unborn of cosmic energies and barren of artistic flower. The cry to the dim gods, cut off from ethics and cosmology, has become mere Psychical Research. Everything has been sundered from everything else, and everything has grown cold.... This world is all one wild divorce court; nevertheless, there are many who still hear in their souls the thunder of the authority of human habit; those whom Man hath joined let no man sunder.[8]

Here Chesterton was speaking again of the traditional, accumulated wisdom of humanity, which was nowhere more faithfully preserved than in the Christian church and its scriptures and creeds.

There was a notion, popular in Chesterton's time as it is today, that to believe in a traditional creed is synonymous with placing one's mind in a prison. Chesterton hastened to argue that nothing could be farther from the truth. Writing of his own experience, he said, "It is only since I have known orthodoxy that I have known mental emancipation."[9] This emancipation G.K.C. meant not only in a personal sense, but also in a larger, sociological and historical sense:

> [O]rthodoxy is not only (as is often urged) the only safe guardian of morality and order, but it is also the only logical guardian of liberty, innovation and advance.[10]

We have seen Chesterton's evidence and arguments to support this view in the previous chapters.

Indeed, this theme of liberation—whether physical, intellectual, or spiritual—is one of the very strongest in the entire compendium of Chesterton's works, both fiction and nonfiction. Liberation was a key issue in his many and varied treatments of the meaning of madness. It was a key issue in all of his political writing. It surfaced repeatedly as a key issue in his journalism. And the case could hardly have been otherwise, for Chesterton's very conception of God and his philosophy of humanity took the free will of the human being as a foundational article of faith. In this regard he wrote,

> The idea of liberty has ultimately a religious root; that is why men find it so easy to die for and so difficult to define. It refers finally to the fact that, while the oyster and the palm tree have to save their lives by law, man has to save his soul by choice.[11]

Chesterton considered anything that sought to deny people the possibility of choice to be not only inhuman, but evil. In writing about symbolism in art, he stated that "it was a wise instinct by which heaven was symbolized by wings that are free as the wind, and hell symbolized by chains."[12] Thus, far from being about locking people's minds in an intellectual prison, orthodox doctrine is about the most profound liberation that human beings can possibly imagine.

The Apostles' Creed begins with the fact of God, the Creator of heaven and earth. Being literally the first article of Christian faith, this fact of God necessarily impacts the entire cosmos of things and ideas, body and spirit. It clearly rejects any materialist notions of the cosmos merely happening by a series of accidents or the unfolding of mechanistic laws. On the other hand it clearly rejects any metaphysical notions that our material existence is merely an illusion or a product of our perceptions or other states of consciousness. Christian doctrine holds that there is a Creator, and there is that which is created.

It follows that the Creator is infinitely greater than the creature. G.K.C. pointed out that

> When once a god is admitted, even a false god, the Cosmos begins
> to know its place: which is the second place.[13]

We have seen that Chesterton was particularly distressed by any claims of human omnipotence, as well as by any theories that subordinated the human will to inexorable "laws of nature." He felt that it was of supreme importance to distinguish always between the Creator and the things created.

As we saw repeatedly in earlier chapters, one of the most pivotal tenets of Christian doctrine for Chesterton was that men and women were specially created in the image of God. We have already examined many of the social, political, and philosophical consequences of this fact in Chesterton's thought, but we need here to place this essential doctrine in its theological context. For upon that phrase, "in the image of God," rests the cornerstone of G. K. Chesterton's theology.

Here is a doctrine that definitely places humanity in a subordinate and dependent position with regard to the Creator, and yet it is a doctrine that ascribes to men and women a level of intrinsic dignity unequaled among created things. In fact, so special is this relationship between God and human beings that G.K.C. was moved to write,

> [E]arth is not even earth without heaven, as a landscape is not a
> landscape without the sky. And in a universe without God there
> is not room enough for a man.[14]

This sentiment includes not only humanity's unfathomable need for God, but also an inference of the very unique relationship between God and these creatures formed in God's image. It is a miraculous relationship, which an individual human is entirely capable of perceiving. In his *Autobiography* G.K.C. described this perception:

> I find myself ratified in my realisation of the miracle of being alive; *not* in some hazy literary sense such as the sceptics use, but in a definite dogmatic sense; of being made alive by that which can alone work miracles.[15]

One of the many things that make the human creature unique is the ability to appreciate the miracle of the human being.

An important consequence of being specially created in the image of God is a basic human dignity, which carries with it certain basic rights. In social and political terms, as we have seen, Chesterton felt that this dignity called for a certain level of justice, of freedom, and of the means of subsistence for every person. In Chesterton's view, to exploit or degrade any man or woman is to do so to the very image of God, and Chesterton's sacramental view gives even more literal meaning to Jesus' famous words "to the extent that you did it to one of these brothers of Mine, even the least of them, you did it to Me."[16] In Chesterton's thought, here was the initial point of connection between Christian doctrine and human rights. "When people begin to ignore human dignity," he wrote, "it will not be long before they begin to ignore human rights."[17]Another important consequence of our being created "in the image of God" is that human beings are created capable of making moral choices. This aspect of humanity is one of the least adequately recognized or explained by the modern human sciences, which tend either to deny the capability altogether or to relativize the moral dimension out of existence. But again Chesterton accused the scientists of ignoring important facts—in this case the fact of the human soul and the fact of sin. In his book, *Heretics,* he wrote about

> ... the great scientific fallacy; I mean the habit of beginning not with the human soul, which is the first thing a man learns about, but with some such thing as protoplasm, which is about the last .... If he had begun with the human soul—that is, if he had begun on himself—he would have found original sin almost the first thing to be believed in. He would have found, to put the matter shortly, that a permanent possibility of selfishness arises from the mere fact of having a self, and not from any accidents of education or ill-treatment.[18]

And recall his comment in *Orthodoxy:*

> Modern masters of science are much impressed with the need of beginning all inquiry with a fact. The ancient masters of religion were quite equally impressed with that necessity. They began with the fact of sin—a fact as practical as potatoes.[19]

Not to belabor the point, but to share some of Chesterton's more colorful comments on the subject, here is a rendition from one of his journal essays:

> If I beat my grandmother to death to-morrow in the middle of Battersea Park, you may be perfectly certain that people will say everything about it except the simple and fairly obvious fact that it is wrong. Some will call it insane.... Some will call it vulgar, disgusting, and the rest of it.... Others will talk about the loathsome spectacle.... Another school of thinkers will say that the action is lacking in efficiency.... The only real point that is worth mentioning is that the action is wicked, because your grandmother has a right not to be beaten to death.... It will call the action anything else—mad, bestial, vulgar, idiotic, rather than call it sinful.[20]

The Christian doctrine of original sin is essential to the theology of Jesus as the Christ and Savior of the world. This doctrine comes from the Genesis story of Adam and Eve, the temptation, and the fall. In Chesterton's writings, its central importance lay in the establishment of humanity's intrinsic propensity to sin—to such very human traits as selfishness, greed, lust, pride, and other forms of curruption. The Christian view of humankind is one of true equality—that everyone is equally capable of wickedness. In one of his novels, G.K.C. wrote, "Man is a contradiction in terms; he is a beast whose superiority to other beasts consists in having fallen."[21] Similarly, in *Orthodoxy* he wrote,

> In one way Man was to be haughtier than he had ever been before; in another way he was to be humbler than he had ever been before. In so far as I am Man I am the chief of creatures. In so far as I am *a* man I am the chief of sinners.[22]

At a first encounter in a superficial sense, this doctrine of the sinfulness of humanity may appear to be a rather pessimistic assessment of the human condition. This particular doctrine is without a doubt the most unattractive to modern sensibilities; and yet, G.K.C. would argue that attractiveness is hardly the point.

> But Christianity preaches an obviously unattractive idea, such as
> original sin; but when we wait for its results, they are pathos and
> brotherhood, and a thunder of laughter and pity; for only with
> original sin can we at once pity the beggar and distrust the king.[23]

To pity the beggar and distrust the king is to reject outright all
notions that some certain people are more trustworthy and valuable
than others.

Theologically speaking, original sin puts all people in the same
sinking vessel with the same need to be saved from the consequences of their selfishness. In this sense, original sin gives meaning
to the gospel, or good news, of Jesus the Christ. It is the foundation
for the revolutionary—though often ignored—Christian doctrine
that kings and beggars have the same rights and responsibilities
before God. It is the framework for Christians' two greatest commandments—to love God and to love our neighbors.

To illustrate and vivify this Christian doctrine of the creation
and fall of humankind, Chesterton wrote a play called *The Surprise*.
Here G.K.C. probed some of the possible purposes or motives of
the Creator in endowing human beings not only with an intelligent
mind, but even more importantly with a free will.

The Surprise is a delightful play, which Chesterton wrote in 1932
but which was not published until long after his death. It is a play
containing two plays within it; G.K.C. used this vehicle to contrast
human beings in their ideal or best state versus human beings in
their fallen state. This method also enabled him to offer some insight
into why the Creator made human beings in the first place.

The play begins with a Friar happening upon a traveling stage
show and at first mistaking the very lifelike puppets for real human
beings. There ensues a conversation wherein the man who made
the puppets and wrote their play—called the Author—persuades
the Friar to stay and watch his little play, which is called "The Surprise." The Author explains that he wrote the play on a bet that he
could not write an interesting story without a villain:

> It seemed as if all virtue was really produced by villains. Well, he
> betted me I could not write a play without a villain. . . . But I swore
> I would do more than that. I swore I would make a whole play,
> not only of good people, but of good actions. In that play, not
> only is there not a single villain, but there is not a single deed of
> villainy. . . . In short, I mean, they all behaved handsomely ac-

cording to their lights. They were all at their best. Everyone behaved well.[24]

To G. K. Chesterton this question of joy and adventure in life without villainy was not an incidental question. It was a question raised in his novel *Manalive* and elsewhere in his writings. It was important to G.K.C. that people understand the falsity, the heresy, in the popular notion equating fun with badness. One of his most persistent themes was that the greatest fun, the highest adventure, the deepest joy is to be acquired through humility and goodness.

And so the Friar and the Author watch the stage play as the Author's very realistic puppets play out their parts as he has designed them to do. The story is a simple one—the details of which I shall not here divulge for fear of ruining the pleasure of reading the play itself—in which there is indeed suspense and surprise and goodness throughout.

And of course, in classic Chestertonian manner the play is full of meaningful lines wherein G.K.C. makes his jabs at the popular fallacies of the day. As only one example, with regard to the erroneous idea that tradition and authority are inimical to freedom, he has one of his characters say,

> Obedience. The most thrilling word in the world; a very thunderclap of a word. Why do all these fools fancy that the soul is only free when it disagrees with the common command? . . . Why should mere disagreement make us free? I know you are fond of dancing; do you want to dance to a different tune from your partner's? You are a fine horsewoman; do you want to think of walking northward all by yourself, when you and your horse are going southward together?[25]

Chesterton was always careful to point out that simply going against tradition and authority is not the same thing as freedom.

But as the little stage play comes to an end and the Author continues to discuss his play with the Friar, the Author begins to complain that there is something more that he longs for—that there is something more he wants for his characters. As he is not making himself perfectly clear, the Friar asks,

Friar: Do you want them to do wrong?

Author: No–No! They could do right. They would do right. They have it in them to do exactly what they do in the play, these people

I know so well. They have it in them . . . and yet they have nothing
in them.[26]

Now we begin to see what Chesterton is getting at with regard to
the Creator and humanity. All of the creation was good as far as it
went, but in order to take full pleasure in these very special creatures
called men and women, there was a need for something more. In
the play the Author laments,:

> Ah, that is the tragedy of the author indeed. Why, they only existed
> because I wanted to get them out of my mind. I wanted them
> separated from me and my life and living lives quite different and
> entirely their own. . . . My whole purpose in making these per-
> sonalities was to put them away from me—to put them a long
> way off, where I could look at them from outside. But where have
> I put them? They exist. They have minds of their own. Why have
> they not got wills of their own?[27]

Then comes the turning point in Chesterton's play; the Author
gets his wish, and his characters come to life with wills of their own.

> Friar: Yes, you have seen your wish come true. You have put them
> outside yourself. They have wills of their own; they are living lives
> of their own.
>
> Author: I only wanted my play—
>
> Friar: It is their play now. Do you remember telling me I might
> call up a hippogriff or some monster from the land of miracles?
> The most monstrous of all monsters are marching across your
> stage, shaking the earth like dragons and chimeras; the most tow-
> ering, the most terrible creatures that life ever let loose upon
> chaos. Stand back—stand out of their way. They are living men.[28]

And so, the second play within Chesterton's play begins. The
beginning plot is the same as the first, the characters are the same,
but this time they have free wills of their own. And this time they
do not act out their best selves, but they display all of the human
failings of selfishness, unkindness, spite, opportunism, pride, and
malignant power over others.

In this flawed version of the stage play the pride and selfishness
of the characters is summarized in the words of the King:

> When will and fate are one, then only is a man a god; and this is
> my hour of godhood.[29]

157

This theme of humans pretending to godhood by dressing their own selfish desires in the cloak of fate recalls much of what Chesterton wrote with regard to economics and politics. In his play *The Surprise* he thus illustrates the essence of fallen humanity: the proud and self-serving rebellion against the Creator and the subsequent philosophies, ideologies, theories and systems designed to justify the rebellion.

As the Author watches in horror as his rebellious characters act their worst, turning a good story bad, bringing grief and violence upon themselves, he comes at last to a point when he can stand it no longer. And on the stage the Author's head bursts through an upper part of the background scenery, and in exasperation the Author proclaims, "[W]hat do you think you are doing to my play? Drop it! Stop! I am coming down."[30]

Here is a new and interesting light on the incarnation of God. Chesterton's play invites us to contemplate an understanding and sympathetic Creator, who endowed us with all of the equipment and abilities to act the play correctly, but who also chose to set us apart by giving us a free will to act on our own. And then on the stage of history we chose to rebel, to act our parts according to our pride and selfish gain, continuing in this way until we had muddled the whole story into a chaos of pain, reaction, and violence. Finally appalled and angered, and yet moved by compassion, the Creator burst into the scene of history—"I am coming down"—and came upon the stage to set things right again. Here is the Christian doctrine of the incarnation in Jesus of Nazareth.

Chesterton's choice of title for his play was far from frivolous, for one of his incessant points was that the story of Jesus Christ is in every way a surprise. The gospel, the story of God incarnate in Jesus of Nazareth, is seen as the greatest surprise of history. In this connection Chesterton wrote,

> The Christian gospel is not a system; a system is fit for turnips.
> The Christian gospel is literally a story; that is, a thing in which
> one does not know what is to happen next.[31]

Chesterton called the Christian gospel a story, as opposed to a system. In his book *Orthodoxy* he explained further,

> All Christianity concentrates on the man at the cross-roads. The
> vast and shallow philosophies, the huge synthesis of humbug, all

talk about ages and evolution and ultimate developments.[32]

But Christian doctrine holds that when it comes to men and women, nothing is inevitable. Chesterton once spoke of "the note of the inevitable; a thing abhorrent to Christians and to lovers of liberty."[33] Being created with a free will and the ability to make moral choices, people are seen as always capable of surprising and unpredictable actions, and as such they will forever elude the predictions of the nomothetic sciences. Even more importantly, here the apparently dismal doctrine of the fall comes to fruition in the greatest optimism of all: that every human being is capable of making the choice that will change the story of his or her life completely and radically in ways that no one would have expected.

Of course the core of Christian doctrine—and the heart of the Apostles' Creed—is the Christ. The creed itself gives a nutshell version of the story of Jesus, the man who was literally God personified. Chesterton described the creed as "a creed which postulates a humanized God and a vividly personal immortality,"[34] because it not only establishes Jesus as one with God, but also speaks of the literal reality of his victory over death.

To Chesterton it was very important to stress that Christ was man and God at the same time. He explained,

> For orthodox theology has specifically insisted that Christ was not
> a being apart from God and man, like an elf, nor yet a being half
> human and half not, like a centaur, but both things at once and
> both things thoroughly, very man and very God.[35]

And then as if to make the gospel story an even greater surprise, this man-God was executed on a cross like a common criminal, and then was resurrected in bodily form on the third day thereafter.

The meaning of the resurrection is that there is reason for hope—there is a precedent and a method for renewal. There is a way to break out of the self-centered cycles of sin and to begin anew with a cleansed soul and a clear conscience. If the gospel is a story, it is surely a mystery story. For it contains the mystery of repentance, forgiveness, and renewal, which constitutes the basis for Christian hope and good news for all people.

In his *Autobiography* Chesterton recalled his answer when people asked him why he joined the church:

[T]he first essential answer, if it is partly an elliptical answer, is, "To get rid of my sins." For there is no other religious system that does really profess to get rid of people's sins. It is confirmed by the logic, which to many seems startling, by which the Church deduces that sin confessed and adequately repented is actually abolished; and that the sinner really does begin again as if he had never sinned.[36]

And when the Christian has truly confessed and repented for sins, there is an experience of a new life:

He believes that in that dim corner, and in that brief ritual, God has really remade him in His own image. He is now an experiment of the Creator. He is as much a new experiment as he was when he was really only five years old. He stands, as I said, in the white light at the worthy beginning of the life of a man. The accumulations of time can no longer terrify. He may be very grey and gouty; but he is only five minutes old.[37]

The depth of Chesterton's theology of repentance cannot be appreciated without an understanding of his thoughts on humility. One often finds in his writing passing references to this theme, as in *The Ball and the Cross:*

He felt the full warmth of that pleasure from which the proud shut themselves out; the pleasure which not only goes with humiliation, but which almost is humiliation.[38]

This humiliation of which Chesterton speaks is grounded in his earlier comments about the cosmos "knowing its place." In the case of human beings it is grounded in the realization of one's own shortcomings and then a heartfelt confession to one's Creator. Again, such a perspective does not fit well with our self-centered culture. G.K.C. wrote,

But this laborious method is very unpopular with a generation which thinks that self-assertion is a complete substitute for self criticism.[39]

Most modern popular psychologies promote an easy kind of narcissism, wherein men and women are urged to feel very sure of themselves, but fashionably unsure about external truths. Chesterton complained, "A man was meant to be doubtful about himself, but undoubting about the truth; this has been exactly reversed."[40]

One of the central tenets of Chesterton's faith was that humility leads to joy. He once called humility "the exalting paradox of Christianity" and claimed that it was the very scarcity of humility that rendered modern life so dull.[41] In his book *Heretics* he wrote,

> The truth is, "Blessed is he that expecteth nothing, for he shall be gloriously surprised." The man who expects nothing sees redder roses than common men can see, and greener grass, and a more startling sun.[42]

Thus, the protagonists in many of Chesterton's stories personify a blend of humility and romantic adventure, and virtually all of his stories contain surprises. We have seen that G.K.C. considered choice and surprise to be the very essence of a human life well-lived.

Chesterton's thoughts on humility lead logically into his doctrine of gratitude. Recall the discussion in an earlier chapter regarding the young Chesterton's rudimentary theology based on a minimal level of gratitude. In time these early ideas blossomed into a fully developed guiding principle, or what the mature G.K.C. called "the chief idea of my life."[43] In his *Autobiography* he explained it this way:

> I will not say the doctrine I have always taught, but the doctrine I should always have liked to teach. That is the idea of taking things with gratitude, and not taking things for granted. Thus the Sacrament of Penance gives a new life, and reconciles a man to all living, but it does not do it as the optimists and the hedonists and the heathen preachers of happiness do it. The gift is given at a price, and is conditioned by a confession. In other words, the name of the price is Truth, which may also be called Reality; but it is facing the reality about oneself.[44]

In humility and gratitude we are enabled to free ourselves not only from the guilt of our wrongdoing, but from the prison of our own illusions as to our greatness. In being grateful for the good that is given and done to us, we relinquish the expectations and demands that inevitably leave us disappointed, hurt, and angry. When we cease taking our lives for granted, we begin living our lives more like a story, an adventure story full of surprises.

In the earlier chapter on hearing God's laughter, we have already explored Chesterton's doctrine of gratitude and joy. It remains here only to reiterate how profoundly Chesterton's Christianity was a religion of joy. In his writing he often made passing references to the inseparable connection between his faith and his joy. In *Heretics* he mentioned, "Ultimately a man can enjoy nothing except religion."[45] And in the same context he claimed,

> Great joy does not gather the rosebuds while it may; its eyes are fixed on the immortal rose that Dante saw. Great joy has in it the sense of immortality; the very splendour of youth is the sense that it has all the space to stretch its legs in.[46]

Likewise in *Orthodoxy* he explained,

> The mass of men have been forced to be gay about the little things, but sad about the big ones. Nevertheless . . . it is not native to man to be so. Man is more himself, man is more manlike, when joy is the fundamental thing in him, and grief the superficial. Melancholy should be an innocent interlude, a tender and fugitive frame of mind; praise should be the permanent pulsation of the soul.[47]

And so, we have noted that the great bulk of Chesterton's writings were not what is strictly called "religious" writings. There were few lengthy discussions of theology, and fewer direct references to Scriptures. Most of his work consisted of articles in the newspapers and weekly journals of his time, ranging in topics from modern art to the war in South Africa. And yet in a sense *all* of his writings were religious writings.

For everything Chesterton wrote—from the nonsense verses in *Greybeards at Play* to the sociology in *What's Wrong with the World*—reflected G. K. Chesterton's perspective and vision of how the world was and how the world ought to be. And the perspective of Chesterton was always richly imbued with the humility and gratitude and joy which he derived from his Christian faith. Here are the global themes that colored everything that Chesterton wrote; here is the heart of Chesterton's religion.

G. K. Chesterton was known by his contemporaries as one of the jolliest men alive, and the reader of his essays and stories can surely attest to the author's deep-rooted joy. We have seen that his joy had much to do with gratitude; it had much to do with surprise; it had much to do with the hope of renewal and resurrection. There were times when Chesterton would—if only in passing—pull it all together, such as in his essay, "The Priest of Spring":

162

And when I look across the sun-struck fields, I know in my inmost bones that my joy is not solely in the spring. . . . There is somebody or something walking there, to be crowned with flowers: and my pleasure is in some promise yet possible and in the resurrection of the dead.[48]

Chesterton once speculated that there was one great aspect that God had not shared with us when he walked on earth, "and I have sometimes fancied that it was His mirth."[49] But there was, in fact, one who lived and believed and wrote in such a way as to illuminate God's mirth and show its reality in the traditional creeds of the church and in the everyday lives of men and women in a hurting world. That very special person was Gilbert Keith Chesterton.

Notes

Chapter 1: Discovering Chesterton

1. G. K. Chesterton, *Orthodoxy* (New York: Image Books, 1959), 12.
2. G. K. Chesterton, "The Unfinished Temple" in *What's Wrong with the World* (London: Cassell and Company, 1913), 39.
3. G. K. Chesterton, *Heretics* (New York: John Lane Company 1909), 93.
4. *Orthodoxy,* 125.
5. *What's Wrong with the World,* 206.
6. G. K. Chesterton, *The Thing: Why I Am a Catholic* (London: Sheed and Ward, 1929), 128, 72.
7. G. K. Chesterton, "The Error of Impartiality" in *All Things Considered* (London: Methuen and Company, 1915), 159–60.

Chapter 2: Hearing God's Laughter

1. G. K. Chesterton, "The Common Vision" in *What's Wrong with the World,* 99.
2. G. K. Chesterton, "Spiritualism" in *All Things Considered,* 153–54.
3. G. K. Chesterton, "Cockneys and Their Jokes" in *All Things Considered,* 17.
4. Galatians 5:22–23 in *New American Standard Bible* (Carol Stream, IL: Creation House, 1971).
5. G. K. Chesterton, *Greybeards at Play* (London: Paul Elek, 1974), 58.
6. Ibid., 37.
7. G. K. Chesterton, "The Enchanted Man" in *A Miscellany of Men* (London: Methuen and Company, 1912), 54.
8. G. K. Chesterton, "On the Laureateship" in *All Is Grist* (New York: Books for Libraries Press, 1967), 166.
9. G. K. Chesterton, "On Running After One's Hat" in *All Things Considered,* 31.
10. G. K. Chesterton, *Autobiography* (New York: Sheed and Ward, 1936), 39.
11. G. K. Chesterton, "Oxford From Without" in *All Things Considered,* 77.
12. Ibid., 75.
13. G. K. Chesterton, "Demagogues and Mystagogues" in *All Things Considered,* 178.
14. G. K. Chesterton, "On Experience" in *All Is Grist,* 238.
15. G. K. Chesterton, "The Sectarian of Society" in *A Miscellany of Men,* 117.
16. Matthew 23:4 in *New American Standard Bible.*

17. G. K. Chesterton, "On Condiments and Conduct" in *All Is Grist,* 205.

18. G. K. Chesterton, "The Zola Controversy" in *All Things Considered,* 70.

19. *Greybeards at Play,* 70.

20. G. K. Chesterton, "About Puritanism" in *As I Was Saying* (New York: Books for Libraries Press, 1966), 43.

21. G. K. Chesterton, "On Sightseeing" in *All Is Grist,* 196.

22. G. K. Chesterton, *The Flying Inn* (London: Methuen and Company, 1919), 64.

23. Ibid., 161.

24. Ibid., 33.

25. Ibid., 42.

26. Ibid., 47.

27. Ibid., 157.

28. Ibid., 59.

29. G. K. Chesterton, *Manalive* (London: T. Nelson and Sons, 1915), 5.

30. Ibid, 79.

31. Ibid., 274.

32. Ibid., 275.

33. Ibid., 361.

34. Ibid., 204–205.

35. Ibid., 205.

36. Ibid., 211.

37. Ibid., 218.

38. Ibid., 53.

39. Ibid., 49.

40. Ibid., 60.

41. Ibid., 366–67.

42. G. K. Chesterton, "The Unfinished Temple" in *What's Wrong with the World,* 39.

43. *Manalive,* 5.

44. *Greybeards at Play,* 15.

45. *Autobiography,* 345.

46. *Orthodoxy,* 31.

47. *Heretics,* 164.

48. *Autobiography,* 344.

49. *Orthodoxy,* 55.

50. *Autobiography,* 178.

Chapter 3: Coming of Age in Industrial England

1. *Autobiography,* 134–35.

2. Ibid., 1.

3. Ibid., 22.

4 Maisie Ward, *Gilbert Keith Chesterton* (London: Sheed and Ward, 1944), 13.

5. *Autobiography*, 101.

6. *Greybeards at Play*, 88.

7. Ward, *Gilbert Keith Chesterton*, 26.

8. *Autobiography*, 61.

9. Ward, *Gilbert Keith Chesterton*, 31.

10. *Autobiography*, 172.

11. Ibid., 171.

12. Ibid., 136.

13. Ibid., 88–89.

14. Ibid., 89–90.

15. Ibid., 90.

16. Ward, *Gilbert Keith Chesterton*, 57.

17. *Autobiography*, 97.

18. Ward, *Gilbert Keith Chesterton*, 59.

19. Ibid., 77.

20. Ibid., 77.

21. Ibid., 78.

22. Ibid.

23. Ibid., 62.

24. *Autobiography*, 179.

25. *Greybeards at Play*, 77.

26. *Autobiography*, 231.

27. Ibid., 233.

28. G. K. Chesterton, *The Catholic Church and Conversion* (New York: Macmillan Company, 1926), 30.

29. Ibid., 80.

30. Ward, *Gilbert Keith Chesterton*, 242.

31. *The Catholic Church and Conversion*, 68.

32. Ward, *Gilbert Keith Chesterton*, 397.

33. *The Catholic Church and Conversion*, 107–108.

34. *Orthodoxy*, 154.

35. *The Catholic Church and Conversion*, 105.

36. Ibid., 95.

37. Ibid., 93.

38. Ibid., 86.

39. Ward, *Gilbert Keith Chesterton*, 504.

Chapter 4: Telling a Good Story

1. "On Logic and Lunacy" in *All Is Grist*, 105.

2. *Heretics*, 208.

3 Ibid., 193.

4. G. K. Chesterton, "A Much Repeated Repetition" in *The Chesterton Review*, XIX No.2 (May 1993), 147.

5. *Autobiography*, 339.

6. Ibid., 334.

7. G. K. Chesterton, *The Complete Father Brown* (New York: Dodd, Mead, and Company, 1951), 23.

8. G. K. Chesterton, *The Club of Queer Trades* (New York: Dover, 1987), 33.

9. *Autobiography*, 297–98.

10. Ibid., 298.

11. G. K. Chesterton, *The Victorian Age in Literature* (New York: Henry Holt and Company, 1913), 90.

12. *Heretics*, 192.

13. G. K. Chesterton, *The Napoleon of Notting Hill* (New York: John Lane Company, 1904), 106.

14. Ibid., 274.

15. *Autobiography*, 97–98.

16. Ibid., 100.

17. Ibid., 100.

18. G. K. Chesterton, *The Man Who Was Thursday: A Nightmare* (New York: Dover Publications, 1986), 25.

19. Ibid., 110.

20. G. K. Chesterton, *The Man Who Knew Too Much* (London: Cassell and Company, 1923), 99.

21. Ibid., 116.

22. Ibid., 96.

23. Ibid., 130.

24. G. K. Chesterton, *Tales of the Long Bow* (London: Cassell and Company, 1925), 97.

25. G. K. Chesterton, *The Poet and the Lunatics* (London: Cassell and Company, 1929), 259.

26. Ibid., 63–64.

27. Ibid., 65–66.

28. G. K. Chesterton, *Four Faultless Felons* (London: Cassell and Company, 1930), 153–54.

29. Ibid., 110.

30. Ibid., 155–56.

31. G. K. Chesterton, *The Paradoxes of Mr. Pond* (Philadelphia: Dufour Editions, 1963), 59.

32. Ibid., 74.

33. Ibid., 74–75.

Chapter 5: Resisting the Spell

1. G. K. Chesterton, "The Wind in the Trees" in *Tremendous Trifles* (New York: Dodd, Mead, and Company, 1910), 89.

2. Ibid., 89–90.

3. Ibid., 92.

4. G. K. Chesterton, *The Everlasting Man* (New York: Dodd, Mead, and Company, 1952), 162–163.

5. *Orthodoxy,* 24.

6. Ibid., 60.

7. Ibid., 127.

8. Ibid., 24.

9. "About the Censor" in *As I Was Saying,* 36.

10. *Orthodoxy,* 24.

11. G. K. Chesterton, *Eugenics and Other Evils* (London: Cassell and Company, 1922), 128.

12. *Heretics,* 286.

13. *Orthodoxy,* 152.

14. "Wisdom and the Weather" in *What's Wrong with the World,* 87.

15. *Orthodoxy,* 43.

16. *All Things Considered,* 201.

17. G. K. Chesterton, "On the King" in *Come to Think of It* (London: Methuen and Company, 1930), 234–35.

18. "The Error of Impartiality" in *All Things Considered,* 159.

19. "About Darwinism" in *As I Was Saying,* 197.

20. "The Sultan" in *A Miscellany of Men,* 203.

21. *Heretics,* 227–28.

22. *Manalive,* 56.

23. *Orthodoxy,* 62.

24. Ibid., 77.

25. *Autobiography,* 182.

26. *Heretics,* 263.

27. "On a Humiliating Heresy" in *Come to Think of It,* 150.

28. *Orthodoxy,* 25.

29. "Wine When It Is Red" in *All Things Considered,* 173.

30. "On the Mythology of Science" in *Come to Think of It,* 131–32.

31. "On Dante and Beatrice" in *All Is Grist,* 126.

32. "About Darwinism" in *As I Was Saying,* 198.

33. "On the Mythology of Science" in *Come to Think of It,* 133.

34. *Orthodoxy,* 84.

35. G. K. Chesterton, *The Ball and the Cross* (London: Wells Gardner, Dalton, and Company, 1910), 134–35.

36. "About Impermanence" in *As I Was Saying,* 125–26.

37. "Woman" in *All Things Considered,* 80.

38. *Heretics,* 121.

39. Ibid., 35.

40. *Orthodoxy,* 105–06.

41. Ibid., 107–08.
42. *Heretics,* 36.
43. Ibid., 302.
44. *Eugenics and Other Evils,* 92–93.
45. Ibid., 96.
46. *Heretics,* 33.
47. *Orthodoxy,* 74.
48. "The Case for the Ephemeral" in *All Things Considered,* 9.
49. *The Flying Inn,* 224–25.
50. *Heretics,* 285.
51. "The Fear of the Past" in *What's Wrong with the World,* 32.
52. Ibid., 33.
53. "About Royal Weddings" in *As I Was Saying,* 227–28.
54. *Orthodoxy,* 47–48.
55. "The Fear of the Past" in *What's Wrong with the World,* 34.
56. "About Traffic" in *As I Was Saying,* 27.
57. "About Change" in *As I Was Saying,* 166.
58. "About the Telephone" in *As I Was Saying,* 185.
59. Ibid., 183.
60. Ibid., 185.
61. G. K. Chesterton, *The Ballad of Saint Barbara* (London: Cecil Palmer, 1922), 18.

Chapter 6: Jousting with the Giant

1. *Heretics,* 72.
2. "Science and Religion" in *All Things Considered,* 142.
3. "On Quacks in the Home" in *All Is Grist,* 131.
4. Ibid., 131.
5. "On Gossip About Heredity" in *All Is Grist,* 117–19.
6. "On Quacks in the Home" in *All Is Grist,* 131.
7. *Orthodoxy,* 144.
8. *The Ballad of Saint Barbara,* 82.
9. "On Gossip About Heredity" in *All Is Grist,* 117.
10. "On Dante and Beatrice" in *All Is Grist,* 124.
11. *The Flying Inn,* 208.
12. *Heretics,* 171.
13. Ibid., 171.
14. "The False Photographer" in *A Miscellany of Men,* 196, 200.
15. "Science and Religion" in *All Things Considered,* 147.
16. Ibid., 146.
17. Ibid., 147.
18. "On Change" in *Come to Think of It,* 136.

19. "Tom Jones and Morality" in *All Things Considered*, 197.
20. "About Relativity" in *As I Was Saying*, 141.
21. "The Angry Author: His Farewell" in *A Miscellany of Men*, 264.
22. Ibid., 265.
23. "Tom Jones and Morality" in *All Things Considered*, 198.
24. Ibid., 199.
25. "The Error of Impartiality" in *All Things Considered*, 160.
26. Ibid., 160.
27. *Eugenics and Other Evils*, 132.
28. *Manalive*, 59–60.
29. *Autobiography*, 75.
30. Ibid., 76.
31. "About Poetry" in *As I Was Saying*, 76.
32. *Eugenics and Other Evils*, 76–77.
33. Ibid., 77, 85.
34. *Heretics*, 15.
35. Ibid., 23–24.
36. "On Original Sin" in *Come to Think of It*, 157.

Chapter 7: Tilting at Dragons

1. "The Sentimental Scot" in *A Miscellany of Men*, 111.
2. "The Man on Top" in *A Miscellany of Men*, 219.
3. "The Insane Necessity" in *What's Wrong with the World*, 109.
4. "About the Workers" in *As I Was Saying*, 171.
5. "The Sentimental Scot" in *A Miscellany of Men*, 112.
6. *Autobiography*, 19.
7. "The Insane Necessity" in *What's Wrong with the World*, 107.
8. "Oppression by Optimism" in *What's Wrong with the World*, 71.
9. "The Miser and His Friends" in *A Miscellany of Men*, 141–42.
10. Ibid., 142.
11. "The Sectarian Society" in *A Miscellany of Men*, 115.
12. "The Sentimental Scot" in *A Miscellany of Men*, 111.
13. "The Homelessness of Jones" in *What's Wrong with the World*, 75.
14. *Autobiography*, 277.
15. "The Sun Worshipper" in *A Miscellany of Men*, 61.
16. "History of Hudge and Gudge" in *What's Wrong with the World*, 62.
17. *Orthodoxy*, 118.
18. *Autobiography*, 354.
19. "About the Workers" in *As I Was Saying*, 172.
20. "The Homelessness of Jones" in *What's Wrong with the World*, 75.
21. "Oppression by Optimism" in *What's Wrong with the World*, 71.

22. "The Homelessness of Jones" in *What's Wrong with the World*, 78.
23. "The Wildness of Domesticity" in *What's Wrong with the World*, 59.
24. *Greybeards at Play*, 82.
25. "The Voter and the Two Voices" in *A Miscellany of Men*, 44.
26. *Autobiography*, 216.
27. "Conceit and Caricature" in *All Things Considered*, 48.
28. "The Thing" in *A Miscellany of Men*, 10.
29. "The Voter and the Two Voices" in *A Miscellany of Men*, 38.
30. "On Political Secrecy" in *All Things Considered*, 98.
31. *Orthodoxy*, 118, 120.
32. *Heretics*, 167.
33. *Orthodoxy*, 126.
34. "The Wrong Incendiary" in *A Miscellany of Men*, 75.
35. "The Vote and the House" in *All Things Considered*, 37.
36. *The Flying Inn*, 189.
37. "The Voter and the Two Voices" in *A Miscellany of Men*, 37.
38. G. K. Chesterton, "Oxford From Without" in *All Things Considered*, 72.
39. "The Boy" in *All Things Considered*, 119.
40. "The Medieval Villain" in *A Miscellany of Men*, 234.
41. *Orthodoxy*, 126.
42. *Autobiography*, 128.
43. "The Charm of Jingoism" in *What's Wrong with the World*, 84–85.
44. *Autobiography*, 133.
45. "The Charm of Jingoism" in *What's Wrong with the World*, 85.
46. *Autobiography*, 107.
47. Ibid., 128.
48. Ibid., 116.
49. Ibid., 230.
50. *Orthodoxy*, 118.
51. *Autobiography*, 354.
52. "The Free Man" in *A Miscellany of Men*, 78.
53. *Orthodoxy*, 110.

Chapter 8: Consorting in Fairyland

1. *Orthodoxy*, 49.
2. *Autobiography*, 173.
3. Ian Boyd, "Chesterton and C. S. Lewis" in *The Chesterton Review*, XVII, Nos. 3. and 4 (August/November 1991), 308.
4. *Autobiography*, 146.
5. Ibid., 147.
6. G. K. Chesterton, *A Handful of Authors* (New York: Sheed and Ward, 1953), 3.

7. Ibid., 5.
8. G. K. Chesterton, *Magic* (London: Martin Secker, 1913), 45.
9. Ibid., 50–51.
10. Ibid., 61.
11. Ibid., 52.
12. Ibid., 62.
13. Ibid., 60–61.
14. Ibid., 66.
15. Ibid., 67.
16. Ibid., 68
17. Ibid., 72.
18. Ibid., 68.
19. *Orthodoxy*, 51–52.
20. *Magic*, 25.
21. Ian Boyd, "Chesterton and C. S. Lewis" in *The Chesterton Review* XVII, Nos. 3 and 4 (August/November 1991), 308.
22. *Greybeards at Play*, 101.
23. "On the Classics" in *Come to Think of It*, 49.
24. "On Experience" in *All Is Grist*, 193–94.
25. *Heretics*, 191–92.
26. *Orthodoxy*, 10.
27. *Autobiography*, 344.
28. Ibid., 91.
29. Ibid., 345.
30. *Orthodoxy*, 55–56.
31. *Heretics*, 194–95.
32. *Orthodoxy*, 56–57.
33. Ian Boyd, "Chesterton and C. S. Lewis" in *The Chesterton Review*, XVII, Nos. 3 and 4 (August/November 1991).
34. *The Ball and the Cross*, 32.
35. *The Flying Inn*, 171.
36. *Orthodoxy*, 79–80.
37. Ibid., 65.
38. Ibid., 65.
39. *Autobiography*, 294.
40. *Manalive*, 9.
41. *Autobiography*, 132.
42. *Orthodoxy*, 28.

Chapter 9: Getting to the Heart of Matters

1. *Orthodoxy*, 12–13.
2. *The Ball and the Cross*, 87.

3. "The New Hypocrite" in *What's Wrong with the World*, 17.
4. "On the Renaissance" in *All Is Grist*, 160–62.
5. "A Dead Poet" in *All Things Considered*, 206–07.
6. *Orthodoxy*, 143.
7. "The Universal Stick" in *What's Wrong with the World*, 121–22.
8. Ibid., 121–22.
9. *Orthodoxy*, 158.
10. Ibid., 141.
11. "The Free Man" in *A Miscellany of Men*, 77.
12. "On Gossip About Heredity" in *All Is Grist*, 122.
13. "The Priest of Spring" in *A Miscellany of Men*, 96–97.
14. G. K. Chesterton, *The Crimes of England*, (London: Cecil Palmer and Hayward, 1915), 40.
15. *Autobiography*, 353.
16. Matthew 25:40 in *New American Standard Bible*.
17. "On the Laureateship" in *All Is Grist*, 167.
18. *Heretics*, 79.
19. *Orthodoxy*, 15.
20. "The Boy" in *All Things Considered*, 114–15.
21. *The Ball and the Cross*, 10.
22. *Orthodoxy*, 94.
23. Ibid., 157.
24. G. K. Chesterton, *The Surprise* (New York: Sheed and Ward, 1953), 40.
25. Ibid., 30.
26. Ibid., 41.
27. Ibid., 42.
28. Ibid., 45.
29. Ibid., 59.
30. Ibid., 63.
31. "A Much Repeated Repetition" in *The Chesterton Review*, XIX, No.2 (May 1993), 147.
32. *Orthodoxy*, 136.
33. *Autobiography*, 110.
34. "The New Theologian" in *A Miscellany of Men*, 186.
35. *Orthodoxy*, 92.
36. Ibid., 340.
37. Ibid., 341.
38. *The Ball and the Cross*, 24.
39. "On Condiments and Conduct" in *All Is Grist*, 207.
40. *Orthodoxy*, 31.
41. G.K. Chesterton quoted in Ward, *Gilbert Keith Chesterton*, 74.
42. *Heretics*, 65.

43. *Autobiography,* 342.
44. Ibid., 342.
45. *Heretics,* 110.
46. Ibid., 107.
47. *Orthodoxy,* 159.
48. "The Priest of Spring" in *A Miscellany of Men,* 97–98.
49. *Orthodoxy,* 160.

Thomas C. Peters, currently the Educational Careers Coordinator at the University of California, Riverside, holds a Ph.D. in sociology from Southern Illinois University, Carbondale. Beginning as a high school teacher of English and social studies, he also has taught on the college and university level and has served as consultant to the Alfred North Whitehead Center at the University of Redlands.

A committed Christian and Presbyterian elder, Dr. Peters is an avid reader of theology and the history of the church and its theological controversies. He has written an autobiography of his own spiritual journey and lists among his favorite Christian writers Thomas Aquinas, Augustine, Thomas a Kempis, Martin Luther, John Calvin, John Wesley, John Henry Newman, Thomas Merton, G. K. Chesterton, and C. S. Lewis, concluding that orthodox Christianity "presents the most sensible and hopeful approach" for a world in crisis.